TRANSGENDER CHRISTIANITY

A Spiritual Journey To Freedom

G. BASS

TRANSGENDER CHRISTIANITY:

A Spiritual Journey To Freedom

G. Bass

Cadmus
Publishing

CadmusPubli
shing.com

TRANSGENDER
CHRISTIANITY:
A Spiritual Journey To Freedom

DISCLAIMER:
The thoughts, opinions, and expressions herein are those of the author and do not reflect those of Cadmus Publishing LLC. Any similarities to actual events or people are purely coincidental. Names and distinguishing characteristics may have been changed to preserve the identities of any individuals. Published by Cadmus Publishing LLC. P. O. Box 8664. Haledon, NJ 07538

Web: Cadmuspublishing.com
Web: Booksbyprisoners.com
Web: MusicbyPrisoners.com
Facebook.com/Cadmuspublishing
Business email: admin@cadmuspublishing.com
Phone: 360.565.6459

ISBN# 978-1-63751-490-0

Book Catalog Info Categories:
LGTBTQ, Christian

CadmusPublishing.com

Acknowledgements

DEE WEE(BFF), DION, NOOKIE, MISS GREG, PAUL, KEVIN FLYTHE,

LARON TURNER, SEAN BELL, AARON CORELY, RAY RAY, CLEO,

TRACY QUARTERMANE, LIL TRACY, BLACK WILL, MISS DICKEY,

MISS TIPPY, THEODORE, RENEE ST CLUE, BRENT NELSON, J.R.,

MISS KEYS, ANTHONY WALKER, JULIUS, LASALLE, MISS RICKY,

VALERIE AND VANESSA, TRIXIE, TERRENCE LEE, PATRICK, R.B.,

GRACE, BRENDA, JOEY, MICHELLE, LIL BERRY, MISS ELLIS,

MALENA SHAW, ANIVAINI STURAS, DARRELL FOSTER, MISS MICKY,

RUBBERBAND WOMAN DARLENE, VENOID, ICE T, JESSICA, F.K.,

SIMONE, CHICAGO MICHAEL, MEMOREX, LIL TONY, LELA, EMORY,

ARNEL, KEISHA A.K.A. JEFFREY MERRIWEATHER, BELINDA,

MISS DETROIT NATALIE, ANDRE MOORE, RAMMER TONY, DEVAUL,

EARTHY KIT, DEWAYNE CONNLEY, DEWAYNE MOHENRY, RUDY EPPS,

TONYAH, MISS GEORGE, DERRICK GIBSON, TWANNA GOLD, TERRY,

TONY RANDOLPH, MISS SEAN (JASMINE), RICKY AND RONNIE,

D.J.: DEJAVUE, JERMAINE (TED'S SON), ERIKA CARTER, MS. GLEN,

D.J. KEN COLLIER AND GREG, LAMARCIS THOMAS,

RAYMOND SOLOMON,
MICHAEL JENNINGS, MELVIN HILL, DA DA, ROCKER,
KENNY, AND
MELBA MOORE... AND IF I FORGOT YA KNOW THAT YOU ARE IN
MY SINCEREST PRAYERS!

NO PLAGIARISM! NO SHADE!

Introduction

A spirit in distress cries out in the wilderness
of turbulent times. A plea that carries the sound
of gloom and agony, filled with pain,
intellectualizing the sorrowful melody of life's intricate
battle. It's "G," a soldier in the trenches of
existence, testifying on behalf of the LGBTQI
Community through the lens of Transgender
Christianity.

Let Us Pray:

Heavenly Father, from the quiet sanctuaries of
our mother's womb. You saw us, our unformed fetus
twirling, and in the Book of Life, all our days
were numbered before we even took our first breath.
The hands of the Divine were already fashioning our
days, our purpose, and our destiny. Dear Lord, thank
you. In your presence, I find myself embraced by
a truth that transcends time and space. I praise
thee because I am fearfully and wonderfully made.
Your works are unique. I know that full well. I
embrace this newborn life, recognizing the most
intricate weaving of the Most High through the
fabric of Salvation.

Foreword

Now let this be an eye-opener to you as "you"
journey into the awareness of God's Presence. Let
us be reminded that in our imperfect world
there are adversaries, those that plot against us,
but in the midst of it all, we hold fast to our
faith in Jesus, for we know that the Almighty is
our protector, our advocate, and our shield.

As you unfurl the pages of this book, please
expect to be enlightened in your mind and spirit.
Pray that we continue to walk by faith and not by
sight, guided by the wisdom of God. Pray that
Grace shields us from the snares set before us as
we invoke the Lord's Presence. O, Lord God, please
permeate our hearts with sensitivity, deep
respect, and an openness to diverse perspectives
regarding the intersection of faith and gender
identity. With no further ado, in the most precious
and Holy name of Jesus, I present...

Transgender Christianity

TABLE OF CONTENTS

CHAPTER 1: DAWN OF REST

This was my awakening, the first step of
faith on a path no longer paved with brittle stones
of nervousness and doubt but with the solid
assurance the risen Christ has set me free. Sunday
morning when I first stepped through the doors of
the church for the very first time, the weight of
my heart was like a stone cast into the depths of
an unfathomable sea--sinking, drowning in self-
awareness and ingrained in perceptions. I saw every
eye upon me as a judgment, every whispered prayer
a condemnation of who I was. I was a sojourner,
seeking sanctuary, but besieged by the profound
apprehension that my sexual orientation, the outward
testimony of my identity, and a life lived
outside the righteous lines drawn in the sand could
ever find home in a place so hallowed.

As I listened the simplicity of the scripture
that promised a yoke easy and a burden light was
foreign to my understanding. "Come unto me all ye
that labor and are heavy laden, and I will give
you rest," He proclaimed but that 'rest' seemed
a concept designed for others, not for me. How
could I, with my catalog of hidden doubts and
displayed deviances, embrace a rest I knew not?
It was a language of the soul I had yet to learn.

The next Sunday I persisted, came again, sat in the back pews, listened to the sermon with a heart cracking open slowly to the possibility of light. It was in this repetition, this returning to the foot of the cross, that I began to discern the multifaceted nature of truth. As my focus had shifted from my own image to the image of the One crucified, the veil that had for so long clouded my perception began to dissipate like mist before the rising sun. I realized that the shackles that fell off were not forged by divine decree but by human interpretation. Interpretations that had me looking at my flaws rather than His grace, my life. style instead of His life, my thoughts instead of - His teachings.

I gradually began to glimpse into the bright essence of true Christianity, not as a religion brimming with rituals and laws, but as a relationship that transcends the boundaries of time and space--a personal communion with Christ Jesus, the Risen. I had first come seeking Jesus the man, the historical figure whose feet graced the dusty road of Galilee. But it was Christ the Messiah, the One who conquered the grave whom I encountered.

In that sacred understanding, I found solace. Imagining his resurrection, declared omnipresence and Ascension eliminated the spiritual geography we inhabited. The arms of the Messiah reach the moon were one to journey so far.

TRANSGENDER CHRISTIANITY—G.BASS

Child of God, hear me now. I come to you on bended knee with this message that is both timely and timeless, rising from the mire of contemporary labels. The ones whose identity treads a path outside the straight lines society has drawn. The one who brings the soft sway of femininity or at other times stand firm in the unyielding posture of masculinity, to the soul who speak in pronouns that dance beyond the traditional, who in jest or fondness, calls another she, he, him, her, girl, miss or ---know that this is 'dedicated to you, the ones who endure the world's ridicule and scorn.

This world, with its quick judgments and sneers hidden behind- thinly veiled glances, knows not the content of one's heart; they perceive not the delicate tapestry of your spirit crafted by the hand of the Divine. But there is One who sees beyond the:-fabrics of flesh and the exhibition of gender expression. The One who gazes directly into the soul---the one and only Jesus Christ.

Think back for a moment in Bethany, nestled in the pages of Holy Scripture where society stood • still to reflect of such a divine encounter. In Mark chapter 14 verse 9 spoke about a woman whose deeds would be forever remembered. This woman, considered the lowest among her people, a known prostitute, found herself at the feet on Our Savior. There in Bethany within a 'Pharisee home, this woman dared to do what tradition forbade. First she let her hair down which Jesus looked at as a sacred act, a vulnerable gesture of devotion.

"She anointed Jesus feet?". Oh the Pharisee, he turned up his nose in disdain, his lips pursed in silent protest, his eyes narrowed with a judgment unspoken trying to indicate to Jesus "Look a dirty sinner touches you, a prostitute at that pollutes you. But Jesus, with compassion infinite and understanding fathomless, looked beyond her status beyond her flesh for in her gesture of humility he saw her heart laid hare her spirit yearning for Grace.

You must understand, beloved, just as the Pharisee failed to comprehend the-true nature of the true nature of that woman's offering, so too does the world fail to comprehend the beauty of your existence. Just as he missed the purity of her worship, so to does the world miss the purity within you. They see your exterior, the fluidity with which you carry yourself, the spectrum of your expressions which they do not understand. But the Lord sees you. You are not unclean in His eyesight.

Rather you decide to embrace the newly defined transgender label is not a barrier to the Most High So if you are one who moves through life feeling neither bound by masculinity nor solely effeminate': or if your soul is a divine blend of both know that you are seen, you are recognized and you are loved. For Jesus is the same today, yesterday and forever He look not at what you wear but what you bear within. So when you find yourself demeaned

remember Jesus who likened Himself to the outcast
the marginalized, the proverbial 'least of these'.
Understand the ridicule of men is nothing compared
to the affirmation of Christ. Duly note, the
Blessed are you when people insult you, persecute
you or falsely say all kinds of evil against you
because of Jesus. "Take heart. for He has overcome
the world and in Him you too shall rise
above the taunts and jeers."

The Kingdom of Heaven, a, realm of unending
acceptance, awaits you, not to be earned by adherence
to cultural standards but to be received
through faith in Christ Jesus. You are invited
not just to witness His grace but to step into
a life drenched in Grace.

Family wears your label or cast it aside
dress as you will Jesus arms is outstretched
ready to embrace you. Let no one dismiss you and
let no laugh cut you deep we are all offered a
place at His table. Your soul has a purpose and
it can find rest if you decide to follow the
footsteps of the Nazarene. Therefore walk boldly
in who you are for the Lord our God is with you
wherever you go. Your Savior died and rose again
not for one type of person but for us all. His
love knows no bounds. He saw the anointing at
Bethany and called it all good and He sees you
now--all of you--and call you too His own. Be
Blessed.

CHAPTER 2 RAINBOWS AND REVELATIONS

Beloved, have you ever stood outside after a storm? Felt the droplets of heaven's tears kissing your visage? Then witness the majestic arc of colors stretched across the sky. That rainbow, the painted banner across the heavens is like God's own smile curving down to touch the earth. Full of beauty and promise. It's like a reminder of the Almighty giving us a wink and reminding us that "I got you".

When God set his rainbow in the sky it was an everlasting covenant between God and every living creature. God's way of saying "I will remember". A symbol of mercy and hope, an umbrella of divine reassurance for all of us walking this sod.

Now fast forward thousands of years after Noah had sailed that oh so crowded boat with a zoo on the water for longer than any cruise you'd ever want to take to a world bursting with colors of another kind. And who's taken up the rainbow in their stride? The LGBTOI± community. Why? Because the symbolism of the rainbow is as rich and diverse as humanity itself. Color represents diversity, inclusion, acceptance and the beauty of blending differences into a tapestry that makes the angels get up and shout "Hallelujah!"

Now let me sprinkle a little humor on this kaleidoscope of truth. You ever notice how a rainbow shows up when you least expect it? Huh? Same with God always showing up with promises in the most unexpected times. So what's the point? Its when God paints the sky with his wide brush of colors the LGBTQI± community are included with its vibrant hues to the human story of help when we need that reminder to love or be loved. It's as if God is telling us "You thought I could work only through shades of your liking. Now watch this as an LGIITQI+ member give help in no way you would imagine as a vessel for Jesus mysterious plans."

That's God signature move when you thought you had it all figured out about who God is going to use and then --barn-- the script gets flipped and help arrives as a reminder for all of us that its power when we unite. I truly believe that each time a rainbow arches across the sky, its God's way of reminding us that his love knows no boundaries. So from now on when you see the rainbow splashed across the sky or waving on a flag pole, proudly take a moment to reflect on how God is working behind the scenes utilizing his people. God is no ordinary artist--no siree-- Remember that rainbow? That's Gods colorful conversation with you, a divine nudge that says, "Keep on keeping on. You're a part of my plan."

CHAPTER 3 THE SPIRITUAL TRANSFORMATION

In the depth of human wandering, far beneath the surface where light seems unrelenting and hope appears to be a fleeting whisper, there resides a profound truth that has been proclaimed from the mountaintops and into the valleys of human suffering: "The longer you go without (food) spiritual nourishment, the more evil will consume your mind." Imagine, if you will, a soul parched like an arid desert waiting for drops of rain. Rain that may seem as distant as the stars above.

This is the plight of many who have wandered away from the oasis of the spirit. It is as though they are caught in a mire of darkness, and with every step fading away from spiritual nourishment further ensnared by the tendrils of evil thoughts and intentions.

But Hark! There comes a promise, a beacon of hope in the wilderness of despair. It comes in the form of spiritual infusion. A boost, a revival, a transaction in the spiritual realm that is invisible to the naked eye and resonates with the power that can shake the foundation of any soul. It's the power of the Church, of collective prayer of meetings where hands are clasped and hearts are united in divine purpose. Where Christ said he would build his church on this rock and not even the gates of hell will prevail against it.

My dearest friends and family as we stay committed and partake consistently in this spiritual nourishment something miraculous begins to unfold. Layer by layer, the attributes of Satan... greed, hate, division etc. are peeled away from the fabric of our being. They are cast aside, and in their place something beautiful, emerges. It is the fruit of the spirit that begins to mature within us.

Ah, yes! The bitter roots of our former selves-- the slut, the tramp, the freak Cannot withstand the light of our newfound reflection. We start to view ourselves with a different lens. One that is not clouded nigh the steam of our past indiscretions. It is a lens that grants us a view of dignity, of self-respect and most important of change.

Understand this: the metamorphosis will not occur in the blink of an eye. It is a process, one that requires patience, perseverance and a commitment to the journey ahead. And yes, labels such as gay, may still linger like shadows at dawn but they do not define us. We must see our past as a testimony a fight fought and a victory won.

The church as it stands is not just a building, a

location, or a gathering place The church is
a spiritual hospital that accepts all regardless
of race, gender, color or nationality the church
will provide the spiritual feast to heal the
ravages of life's illnesses. Therefore every soul
that steps through its doors may be in dire need
of emergency care some an their spiritual death
bed but its the church with the love and understanding
needed to cure the battle scars of life.

Once you come into this spiritual place of
refuge we must ensure our spiritual fruits remain:
ripe for the picking, pluckable by those in need.
For among us walk those whom society has cast
aside-- like the transgender individuals who, by
their very nature, often carry an instinctive will
to help and to heal. Yet, many have deterred them
turned them away by misconceptions of scripture
or by tales of an ancient time where stones were
the hands of judgment and mercy was nothing but a
dim light.

Today, though, the stones are not of rock, but
of words--words that slice through spirits like
assault rifles, words that are wielded with the
intent to destroy any who dare to follow Christ.
Its in such a world that we must STAND FIRM
against the wiles of the enemy.

But be of good courage! For as followers of Christ we are called to stand in the gap to be the wall that shelters the demon possessed who without remorse perform devious acts on a normal basis. We, the church are to be the healers that bind wounds , that offer solace in the face of tyranny, that carry love as a banner in the war against spiritual disrespect.

Wherefore let us be vigilant, for the enemy prowls around like a roaring lion, seeking to devour. Yet he will find no purchase among us, for our armor is forged in divine might, and our weapons are not carnal but mighty through God to the pulling down of strongholds.

In this journey let not your hearts be troubled. Hold fast to the spiritual sustenance that will renew your minds, transform your lives and deliver you from the grip of evil. Take each step daily with the assurance that with every prayer, every meeting, every sermon absorbed is the true essence of who you are in Christ is being unveiled. Take heart for in the Spiritual Hospital there is a bed for you. There is healing there is love and there is transformation. In time the sour taste of promiscuity will be replaced with the sweet satisfaction of purity. Let us then rise like trees planted by the waters our fruit flourishing for all to see we have indeed been with Jesus.

CHAPTER 4 EMBRACING A GOSPEL OF INCLUSIVITY

As I embark upon this sensitive and profound topic within the context of transgender Christianity it is with a great sense of humility to open your hearts to a message that transcends our bitter differences and unites us in the love of Christ. T. come before you not to dwell on historical disputes or divisive rhetoric but to share a word that embraces every child of God regardless the paths they have walked or the identities they hold dear.

In the book of Galatians, the apostle Paul reminds us, "There is neither Jew nor Gentile, neither slave nor free, nor is there male and female, for you are all one in Christ Jesus" Galatians 3:28. This is the message we must hold tr, close because the unity in Christ supersedes all earthly distinctions.

We are living in times where the thread of our society is woven with intricate fabric--threads of diverse cultures, identities and lived experiences. Among these is the LGBTOI± community. Souls who seek to live authentically in a world that often meets them with intolerance. As followers of Christ it is incumbent upon us to be beacons of love and acceptance.

I want to address a misconception that has caused great division among God's children--its the notion that the people who reside in modern Israel are not the descendants of biblical Israelites. Let us remember that our faith teaches us not to be consumed with lineages and ancestries but rather to focus on the love and grace afforded to us through Christ's sacrifice. The Gospel of our Lord is not confined to a single person, race or nation It is a living testament that extends its arms worldwide offering salvation to all.

In the Book of Romans Paul declares, "For there is no distinction between Jew and Greek. For the same Lord of all, bestowing his riches on all who call on him" Romans 10:12. It is through this lens that we must view our fellow humans recognizing that our true identity is not rooted in earthly labels but in our status as beloved creations of the Most High. Therefore, let us not be consumed with the messengers of history, the genealogies of scripture, not the claims of earthly heritage. We are called to a higher purpose--to bear witness to the truth of God's encompassing love to share the Good News with all to affirm the dignity of every individual. As Christians we must stand firm in our conviction that our faith in Jesus Christ is the mortar that binds us, not the worldly distinctions that threaten to tear us apart.

In the Spirit of Christ's universal church we extend the olive branch to transgenders as part of the broader human journey toward understanding, acceptance and spiritual growth. We must recall that our Savior walked this earth not as a divider but as a unifier--one who dined with forbidden tax collectors, spoke with Samaritans in the face of the Ops., and offered redemption to all in need regardless of what a person thought about him.

So, as we navigate the complexities of identity and beliefs we do this anchored in the promise that in Christ we have been given a new identity--one that transcends cultural divides and temporal concerns. Our priority should not be to parse out the messengers hut to ensure that the message of God's everlasting love reaches every corner of the earth touching every heart that beats for truth and light.

The invitation to Jesus table is not limited by the borders drawn by man. It is an invitation that resounds with the clarity of a divine purpose a calling out to every soul that yearns for a connection and every spirit that seeks refuge and let's not forget the ones whose heart that beats for justice. Jesus Christ remains the solution.

In closing, let us recommit ourselves to a faith that looks beyond the external in Jesus' name Amen!

CHAPTER 5 THE AUTHENTICITY OF THE KING JAMES VERSION ONLY

My beloved family, I find it imperative to share with you a revelation most profound that the Holy Spirit has illuminated in the midst of this spiritual sojourn. This divine insight concerns nothing less than the bedrock of our faith. Christ the crucifixion of our Lord Jesus Christ. In this chapter 1 pose to draw your attention to an issue that has weighed heavily upon my heart.

When we gather getting knee deep in scriptures immersing ourselves in what I recall as living water. I noticed a peculiarity. You see, it has become increasingly prevalent that the use of modern Biblical translation--NIV, New KJV, NLT, among others. While these versions present themselves as more accessible, claiming an ease of readability, I submit to you that within these pages lies a subtlety that cannot be ignored.

Our revered King James Version stands as an exemplar of sacred linguistics, a testament to the divine constitution as it was inspired then. Yet, the contemporary iterations seem to diverge from the original, altering the essence of God's immutable law. These changes, seemingly innocuous, sever the sinews connecting us to the heart of scriptural verity. Why do I confront this?

Beware--I beseech you, therefore, beloved to step into this pivotal truth. In Christ Jesus we find freedom from condemnation. His desire is not to languish in consciousness of sins already nailed to the cross. No, Christ yearns for us to bear fruit, to manifest the potential he has lovingly sown within us.

Consider this-- when a tree is conscious only of the soil it springs from, does it not risk failing to reach towards the heavens from which its sustenance derives? Thus, dwelling on a past of shortcomings will hinder the burgeoning of your spiritual fruit, which the world is meant to know us by our love(fruit).

Now let us examine this scripture closely. Notice in the unblemished tongue of the King James Version Luke 3:8 commands us "Bring forth therefore fruits worthy of repentance." Now, compare this to the New Living Translation which states Prove by the way you live that you have repented of your sins and turned to God" Do you see the focal point of their message is sin. However, true biblical repentance, as depicted in Acts 2:38

declares '...Repent and be baptized every one of you in the name of Jesus Christ..." Here the directive is clear: the change of mind is centered on Christ and the act of baptism is just the living testament to a change of mind about Jesus.

Can you feel the weight of such a declaration It is not a cycle of fleeting regrets: Tt is the irreversible pivot towards a new dawn, wherein Christ is the Lord and Savior of your life. This is the only true repentance that saves. Not something you do. Too often I see souls proclaim repentance only to circle back into the old days repeating a dance that leads them away from the initial salvation.

Our calling is to live, love and to bear fruit that endures. For in that growth lies our testimony and in our testimony lies the power to shift this very atmosphere. May we continue to pursue the Lord with a steadfast spirit and a heart ever seeking his unwavering truth. May God Bless You.

CHAPTER 6 LAYING ON OF THE HANDS

Oh beloved, let me give you a testimony-- a story of faith, redemption and the miraculous power that flowed when God's people laid hands in prayer. Now, picture this man **Turtle** named for his unhurried pace in the Lord, but swift was his spirit in his own accepting the transformation of Christ. A true and amazing walking testimony of a turned around change of mind.

Turtle preached with a fire that could ignite: faith in the coldest of hearts. Through Turtle's faithful ministry many found solace, many found hope and many found Christ. Yes, family, the fruit of his work was evident to all.

But then came a storm, a relapse struck our brother Turtle. Meth, that old serpent, that dealer of lies and bondage, ensnared Turtle once again. The man who stood in the pulpit became the man the world now - whispered about-- a preacher turned captive to his addiction. Oh, the enemy thought he had won. But let me tell you, God was not done with Turtle yet.

In the midst of this trial, Brother G. Bass, the author, himself was facing a crisis. Diabetes a thorn in his flesh since 2009, threatened to claim his feet both of them. The doctor had spoke the word none wished to hear. Amputation. But God had a different report, a different path for this faithful servant. Moved by the spirit Brother G. Bass sought Turtle. Not for counsel, not for a sermon but for the gift, of laying on the hands knowing full well the Power bestowed upon him even in his broken state.

Turtle could have hesitated, could have declined, feeling unworthy, but in the Kingdom of God broken vessels are often the conduit for his glory. They held a foot washing ceremony, a profound act of humility, and upon those feet, Turtle laid his hands, invoking the Spirit of the Lord. Striking was the sight, as he caressed those feet while reciting Romans 10:15 "how beautiful are the feet of those who bring good news."

For three weeks, twice a week, they prayed and through the excruciating pain Brother Bass endured with each step he had unwavering faith. A faith that would not accept the prognosis of man over the Almighty's promises!

And let me tell you the whole truth nothing but the truth. Not only were Brother Bass's feet saved from the grasp of the surgeon's knife, free of infection, but also liberated from the bondage of insulin. Diabetes had to bow its knees to the name of Jesus!

But the miracle was not just for Brother Bass Seeing the power of God working through Turtle's brokenness Turtle found hope again. Witnessing the healing Turtle's faith was reignited. He gave a testament to the church that even in our lowest God can use us for his highest.

For we must remember what First Timothy 4:14 tells us "Neglect not the gift that is in thee, which was given by prophecy, with the laying on of the hands..." Turtle's gift was still there not buried with the weight of his struggle. Oh how gracious is our God the one who turns mourning into dancing the one who turned Turtle's relapse into a revival. For in our weakness His strength is made perfect. Hold fast to this, beloved, hold fast!

CHAPTER 7 ADOPTING A TRANSFORMED IDENTITY IN CHRIST

As we undertake this spiritual journey through the depths of Galatians 2:20, let us open our hearts to the transformative power of this text. It speaks to the very core of our Christian faith and more specifically to the lived experiences of all genders seeking to reconcile their selves back to God.

Scripture says "I am crucified with Christ: nevertheless I live; yet not I, but Christ liveth in me: and the life which I now live in the flesh I live by faith in the Son of God, who loved me, and gave himself for me."

This powerful message penned by the Apostle Paul is a testimony of death and resurrection. Not just of Christ but of ourselves. Herein lies a spiritual paradox where death ushers in life, where loss becomes the inception of the truest gain. This verse should resonate deeply for it r speaks of an end and a beginning.

First let us grasp the sincere weight of being crucified with Christ. This crucifixion is not merely a historical moment but an ongoing spiritual reality. Where we acknowledge to lay down the yoke of worldly perceptions and prejudices and put to death the oppressive theories that have long dictated "are you worthy" or "your place in Gods Kingdom is questionable". Turning Christ Crucifixion into a mockery of "its just for us" but Christ recognize your true self although society may not always see you Christ does. He sees you, knows you and loves you deeply enough to have given himself for you too!

This life that we live now "in the flesh" speaks of the present reality--our daily struggles and joys, or victories and: our vulnerabilities. Knowing our identities are not rooted in societal definitions but in Christ himself. It is he who defines who we are: loved valued and redeemed - children of God.

In this life of faith we learn that our faith does not come from worldly acceptance but from divine admission realizing every moment is an act of faith an affirmation that your lives are sustained not by human validation but by the Spirit's invigorating presence within.

Note, the part •of the verse that says "who loved me and gave himself for me" is a declaration of divine love that has no conditions a love that acknowledges and cherishes each one entirely. To be seen by God is truly--- more profoundly than

any drop the human eye can see. For every seeker
know that this affirmation is a touchstone--
a promise when we look in the mirror that we
ought to see ourselves through the eyes of the
the One who created creation and created us and
sees us as beloved.

In living by faith of the Son of God we come
to recognize that true faith encompasses all of
our total being ---gender identities included.
Have no doubt that as you walk by faith you reflect
diverse magnificence of God's creation by
showcasing the boundless creativity of the One
who designed you.

Dear ones, you are invited to live out this
scripture in the fullness of your journey to see t
your experiences reflected in the death and
resurrection of Christ. So let us proclaim Galatians
2:20 as a declaration of our own crucifixion with
Christ because in this new reality you have been
crucified with Christ. That is the gospel that is,
the Good News. It is within this new life, the
rebirth in faith and love that we are called to I
thrive not just survive. Awake, beloved of Christ!
Rise, for you are living epistles of Christ unending
grace and unyielding love. May you walk in
the fullness of your identity, courageously and
faithfully as you should. May God Bless You!

CHAPTER 8 THE INHERITANCE OF SIN AND
THE GATEWAY TO REDEMPTION

In the quiet corners of our beings, in the silent spaces of our souls, there rests an inheritance as old as Methuselah that binds us to history's first misstep, to the original act of disobedience in the Garden of Eden. It is the SINU branch, an ancestral family tree whose roots are entwined with our very essence) w hose leaves murmur secrets of a fallen nature we all share.

In this lineage, every human, regardless of whether the actual act of sin is committed, is horn with the surname of SIN, the progeny of a fractured heritage.

Let us not be mistaken, beloved, the act of sin was committed by our forebears, Adam and Eve, was not simply a singular transgression lost in the archives of time. No it was the inception of a pervasive spiritual condition that we, their descendants, must carry within us-- the inheritance predisposition to stray from the will of the Creator. We are born -into that--lineage, the lineage that ties us to the father of lies. So unless we are born anew unless we are transformed unfortunately, Satan will remain your father.

In the Book of John chapter 8 verse 44 we are confronted by a truth most sobering: "Ye are of your father the devil and the lusts of your father ye will do." Here, we, are starkly reminded that unless we accept Christ, unless we undergo a spiritual conversion, Satan remains our unfit spiritual patriarch. He is the one whose hushed tone echoes in the chambers of our hearts, seducing us into falsehoods, into living a life contrary to the divine blueprint crafted by God.

But I say unto you, let not despair take root, For as deep as the roots of the SIN branch may go, there is one who descended to the deepest abyss, one who through sacrifice and unblemished love, offered a pathway to be grafted onto a newt lineage, the lineage or righteousness--His name is Jesus Christ. As many have received him to them he gave power to become the sons of God.

By accepting Christ our last name is changed and we are connected into the divine family, heirs to an eternal kingdom where sin and shame no longer describes us.

This rebirth, this renewal, is not something we can achieve through our strength; it is a gift, gracefully extended by the nail scarred hands of the One who knew no sin. Keep in mind

To be born again means to be remade in his Image to see the world not through the dim glass of our limited perceptions but through the vibrant spectrum of his love and his righteousness. It is to change a fleeting identity for an eternal identity. To replace the false promises muttered by the father of lies with the resolute truths proclaimed by the Father of the Light.

Make no mistake the process is not without travail. To be reborn is to surrender, to release the shackles of pride and self and to allow those hands that fashioned the universe to mold our hearts anew. It means to accept that our way are not His ways, our thoughts not His thoughts.

It means to daily die to evil and walk in the newness of life that is only found in Christ Jesus. Therein lies a battle, for our adversary is cunning, weaving webs of deception, masquerading as an angel of light while he lays siege to the souls of men.

Like a crafty serpent, he will continue to lie, deceiving you with illusion that our legacy is our own define. But he is a defeated foe, his final breaths spent on sowing discord and chaos knowing his end is near. He will ply you with falsehoods until your final breath if you let him, but at the precipice of eternity he will divulge his deception by confessing to you that "you" were never meant for damnation but for glory and you blew it!

So, what shall we say to these false beliefs? Shall we continue in bondage and neglect the Grac Or, shall we embrace the freedom procured for us on Calvary's cross? It is time to lay claim to the inheritance that Christ has secured for us, time to live as the redeemed, to carry the name of our Heavenly Father eternally etched upon our hearts. Beloved, cast away the weight of generational sin and don the robe of righteousness because Christ bears the emblem of true kinship and we inherit Christ righteousness.

For in Him, we are not just overcomers; we are more than conquerors. In Him, the SIN branch is severed, and a new branch is budding with all the fruit of the spirit--love, joy, meekness, peace, goodness, faithfulness, gentleness, longsuffering, temperance Against such things there is no law and in such things, we find our true heritage...its a divine lineage as the children of the Most High.

CHAPTER 9 THE UNVEILING OF THE ANOINTING

Child of God, lend your heart to a revelation a mystery that has persisted through the ages, echoing from ancient sanctuaries to the hallowed halls of the modern church--the mystery of the anointing. I speak to you this day not of a concept entangled in theological confusion but of a profound truth that dwells at the core of our calling and identity in Christ Jesus. So journey with me fam as we delve into the heartbeat of the anointing, unfolding its layers like a sacred scroll, baring its power for the end of times.

It came to pass in our pursuit of the Divine as we continued to sit under the torrential down—pour of the preached Word, --- a term, both elusive and resounding, would often leap from the pulpit, stirring the depths of the soul--its the term "anointing" that's quite misunderstood. A word we've heard preached and sung about on a regular basis. A word that we have prayed for, time and time again in prayer. Yet for many, it remains a concept shrouded in mystery, a jewel of spiritual significance.

In my relentless quest for understanding, I discovered that to come to terms with the word anointing one must travel back through the

the corridors of history, back to the days of history back to the days of ancient prophets and kings. To comprehend "anointing" in its fullness open your spirit to the distinction between Old Testament "anointing" and New Testament "anointed."

In the Old Testament anointing was the divine act of setting someone apart. Kings, priests and prophets were drenched in holy oil, symbolically clothed with God's authority for their divine assignment. Consider the anointing of Saul, with the prophet Samuel pouring oil upon his head as found in First Samuel 10:1. This was a prophetic, act, declaring divine equipping for service.

Now pivot with me to the New Covenant where the narrative evolves and focalizes upon Jesus, the Anointed One. Through his life, death and resurrection Jesus fulfilled the offices of king priest and prophet. As the Christ, the Messiah, His very name embodies the fulness of anointing.

As believers, when we confess with our mouth - and believe in our hearts Romans 10:9 we are grafted into this anointing. In that holy instance as it is written in Second Corinthians 1:21 and expounded in John 2:20, 27 we are anointed.

Oh yes, this anointing we speak of transcend mere physical oil; for it concerns our relationship with Christ, saturating us with the very essence of His Spirit. It is the indwelling of the Holy Spirit who arrives without delay, settling within us like the sudden illuminating of a room Once shrouded in darkness. This is not an anointing solely for service, but an enabling force to discern truth, to commune with the Almighty, and. to partake in Divine fellowship.

Do not mistake this for an ephemeral feeling that ebbs and flows with the winds of circumstanc:0 No, the Holy Spirit, our Comforter and Guide, makes a home within us, providing an abiding sense of security and affirmation of our sacred union with the Savior. The Light shines, and darkness comprehends it not.

As the Book of Acts unfold with no definitive end, chronicling the deeds of apostles empowered by the Spirit, let us remember that our own unending narrative continues. The acts of this anointing echoes into eternity, for we are living breathing continuations of that divine saga. Our anointing is a beacon of His presence, a testament to the world that we are His.

empowered and enlightened called to manifest the
Kingdom of God on earth as it is in Heaven. So,
let us walk boldly in this understanding, precious
saints, for the anointing we bear is not of ourselves,
but of Him who called us out of darkness
into His marvelous light. And as we cusp this
anointing, let the oil of His presence so permeate
our being that we can't help but to spill out His
love, His grace and His truth to a world in
desperate need of the Savior.

Rejoice, for the anointing is yours, claimed
at the cross and solidified in your proclamation
of faith. Now as you go forth, let the manifestation
of His anointing in your life be as evident
as the dawning of a new day, for you are anointed
for all the days to come. Amen!

CHAPTER 10 THE HEART'S TRUE CIRCUMCISION

Beloved, I beckon you to hear this profound truth and spread it! A revelation --- of Romans 2:29. Here, the Apostle Paul speaks not with ambiguity, but with divine clarity about the true essence of transformation. Paul declares with boldness that authentic identity in this context, being a Jew is not a matter to be discerned by the physical eyes, nor affirmed by the external rituals we undergo. Rather, it is a spiritual reality rooted in the condition of the heart and sanctioned by the Almighty.

Circumcision of the heart is an internal change that cannot be replicated by human hands or rituals. In ancient times there was a belief that physical circumcision was a gateway to righteousness, a safeguard of salvation. How sorely misunderstood this concept was! For it is not the outward marking of the flesh that denotes one's true standing with the Lord but the inward seal of the Spirit.

And so we come to understand that it is by by the Spirit and not the letter of the law that we find favor with the God. The Spirit breathes life into deep places, infuses grace where there was condemnation, yet illuminates those who were in darkness with the radiant light of Christ's love. As the scripture declares, "whose praise is not of men, but of God." It signifies that our reward, our revalidation and our very purpose flows not from the accolades of this world but from the overflowing wellspring of God's favor.

Let me be clear, the Old Testament Covenant expressed through physical ordinances was but a shadow of the things to come. It served a purpose for its time pointing ahead like a signpost to the Savior who would fulfill the law and usher in a New Covenant drenched in his blood and stamped by His resurrection.

Now, Jesus is the cornerstone, the bridge spanning the chasm between Heaven and Earth. By no deeds, by no triumphs of the flesh, by no adherence to the meticulous letter of the law can we be saved. It is only unequivocally and irrevocably, by the transforming power of Jesus Christ taking residence in our hearts that we are rescued from the pangs of sin and eternal separation from our Creator.

Once connected to Christ, oh yes, the Source of all power, we undergo an exchange that the greatest poets and philosophers spend a lifetime trying to articulate. Our hearts, once stony within is softened as we yielded to the Holy spirit. Like clay in the potter's hands, we are reshaped and molded.

This heart transformation, moves us, alters us, propels us far beyond what we could ever achieve on our own. We start to wield a new position that is not of this world--our place "in Christ." The Holy Spirit cultivates this new birth within us, orchestrating a symphony of change that reverberates through the depths of our soul.

What this means for us today is we must journey deeper, past the external facades and the facsimiles of piety. We must invite Christ into that sacred space within, that he may set up shop and transform our hearts into a stage for his eternal presence.... tap dancing away to the beat, So let us not be swayed by the praise of men, for their words are but a vapor. Let our pursuit be the enduring "well done" from the Father, whose approval is everlasting. No form of outward work no humanly constructed bridge leads to the Father

It is only through the heart indwelt by Jesus, our holy bridge, that we may cross with assurance from death unto life, from earthly to spiritual from embrace of sin to the arms of eternal love.

Hear this clearly and let it settle in your heart. For when the heart is circumcised by the Spirit we become new creations, marked eternally alive in Christ, the heirs of an everlasting Kingdom. May this word resonate within you, stirring the depths of your soul, and guiding you along the path that leads to His glorious presence. Amen!

CHAPTER 11 THE REFINEMENT OF A DIAMOND: HOW PRESSURE SHAPES PURPOSE

Beloved, I want you to fix your mind on the making of a diamond. A process vast in time and intense in pressure. You see, it is not in its initial state that it can reflect the light. No it must endure a process.

As it is with our lives as Christians. Most of you know in the heat of persecution you've felt a world that doesn't always understand the journey you're on. But I want to remind you today that just as the diamond cannot be formed without the heat and the pressure so too our faith cannot be proven without trials and tribulations. James 1:2-4 tells us "Consider it pure joy whenever you face trials of many kinds because you know that the testing of your faith produces perseverance."

While the context of our challenges may differ the purpose they serve in God's greater design remains the same. So take heart, for your identity as a Christian and as one embracing your true self, is being solidified through tribulation after tribulation just like the diamond.

Remember, the diamond's beauty becomes evident only after the rigors it encounters underground. When thrusted up to the light it sparkles with resilience, reflecting its multifaceted journey.

Your life, your story too is a dazzling testament to perseverance and faith. Each time you stand firm in the faith, your truth, with every instance you lean on Christ amidst the pressure, you become a living emblem of transformation---precious in the Father's eyes.

God, the Divine Jeweler, sees the value in the raw and the refined. He recognizes the hidden worth in the carbon--the potential for greatness in its purest form--and he likewise sees the treasure within you. "You" my beloved, are being perfected, not in spite of your identity or experiences but through them all. Notice the Lord does not call the equipped he equips the called and in your equipment i.e.; anointing--lies a brilliant light that can pierce through the darkest chasm of misunderstanding and tolerance.

Therefore, rise up with resolve, for in the language of the earth, pressure is not a sentence to break you, but an invitation to greatness, to shine. The trials of being both transgender and Christian are part of your unique story, and they temper you to reflect God's glory--brilliantly resilient, marvelously crafted and poised to deliver a message of hope and redemption to a world in desperate need of understanding the breadth of God's love.

Your existence is not a contradiction but a confirmation of God's ability to create beauty and strength from the most unexpected places. Through your experiences, through your struggles, you effectively carry forth the astonishing narrative of grace--walking the path of a believer transformed and set apart. for just as a diamond emerges from its trials by fire and force more lustrous than ever before, shall your spirit emerge from the refining stages of your journey with an otherworldly radiance that narrates a love divine and endless.

Stand Firm, and let your life be a testament to the power of love, transformation and renewal. For it is through the trials--through the heat,

the pressure, the encompassing darkness-- that the
diamond within you is forged, decked in grace, re
splendent in purpose and profoundly precious in
the sight of the One who promises to never leave
you or forsake you.

So, my beloved family as you face the heat of
misunderstanding, the pressure of society's norms
and the trials of walking in a world that may not
accept you, stand strong in the knowledge that
you are being refined. Hold fast to Jesus, the
author and finisher of our faith. Look forward
to the moment when you will emerge, not as a
piece of carbon but as a stunning diamond,
reflecting the boundless love and radiant light
of our Lord and Savior. For you are precious in
His sight and He is making something beautiful
out of your life.

Be blessed, be resilient and may the light
of Christ shine ever brightly through you,
through all of us, as we journey on this path
together. Amen!

CHAPTER 12 LIVING TESTIMONY OF A TRUE BELIEVER

Beloved, hark with me into the depths of what it means to live a life that is both rooted in faith and robust in action, let us begin with a fundamental truth - faith and works are inseparable they are the warp and weft of the fabric that makes up a believer's life. "Faith without works is dead." says the scripture, and conversely, works without the underpinning of faith are but hollow, aimless gestures. These are not mere idle statements to be glossed over; they are pillars upon which the Christian Walk stands.

Now, I must tell you, wrapped in the wisdom of the Lord, that all the good you think you are doing, if it is not steeped in the acknowledgment and acceptance of faith in Jesus Christ, it runs the risk of being just dead works. You see, once you receive the transformative embrace of belief your works are no longer just works - they become the fruit, the very evidence of your faith

When the spirit of the living God dwells within you, it propels you into action. And what sort of actions are we talking about?

We're talking about a thirst for fellowship, a hunger to feast upon the word daily, a heart that gives not just occasionally, but unconditionally, a spirit that delights in attending church and prayer meetings and the hands that reach out to assist the poor without reservation.

It troubles my spirit to admit that in our bustling lives, concern for the poor, the downtrodden, has slipped to the periphery of our spiritual consciousness. Family, we must not forget the words of our Savior, who Himself said, "... Ye have done it unto one of the least of these brethren Ye have done it unto me." This is not an optional extra; it is the essence of our belief in practice.

Let me share with you a powerful movement of the Spirit. Time and time again the Holy Ghost will urge you, compel you, until your hands extend in generosity and your mouth overflows with testimony of the goodness of God. True stories of transformation abound, where divine encounters reach across the chasms of hatred and bigotry to touch and heal the most hardened of hearts.

Consider this - it was by no mere coincidence that the Lord placed me before a man whose heart brimmed with racial venom. This same man now stands as a witness, testifying to the redeeming power of Christ's love, his heart changed from one that hated to one that loves his fellow man regardless of color or creed. This is what it means to walk in Kingdom purpose, touching lives in ways that only you by your witnessing.

In the toil of this sacred work, remember, you will find no shortage of judgements and voices ready to criticize or cast doubt. But here is where the gift of discernment becomes your ally. You must discern to whom and how your testimony will be shared. Like the converted gangbanger speaks to the heart of another trapped in the cycle of gang violence, so too can someone of the trans community be a beacon of hope for another who shares in a similar struggle.

Your ministry, your service, will often be birthed from your- trials, your tribulations. It will resonate most with those who can identify with your past pains and struggles; it will have power because your story is a bridge that connect conversations and your transformed life will be the Guide.

Therefore, do not be ensnared by the illusion that the Christian walk is an easy path. No, quite the contrary. The moment you step out of the domain of the enemy and into the eternal Kingdom of our God, you set yourself in direct opposition to the currents of this world. To swim against the mainstream is no easy feat, yet it is precisely this resistance that strengthens us, that refines us, and defines us as true followers of the Way.

Let us then not grow weary in doing good. Let us embrace the full measure of our faith, clothing ourselves in the righteous armor of Christ, so , that our faith may be alive and our works full of purpose. Let us remember that we have been called; not just to believe, but to act, not just to pray but to do - for it is by our love, our works, that the world will know we are His disciples.

In this, let us strive to be the living testimony of a true believer, shining forth the indisputable truth that our faith is ever alive, ever working, through our unending devotion to the works the Spirit has prepared for us. Let this chapter of our lives be written with the indelible ink of active faith, and let our story inspire others to rise, to believe, and to act. For it is in this dynamic union of faith and works that our lives are transformed and our communities are revitalized and our world is changed.

Let's visit a Bible Study that commenced not in the usual manner but ended up a testament to the mighty move of the Almighty! This study was no ordinary meeting. It was a tabernacle where the souls from all walks of life converged that day, unified by the thread of faith sturdy enough to weave disparate spirits into a tapestry of grace.

Now, let not your hearts be troubled, for on this particular eve, the sanctuary's doors swung wide, and lo and behold, look who graced us with their presence, a seeker named Daimond, whose arrival would teach us a most valuable lesson. Yes Diamond emerged, bedazzled not just in name but in form, sporting a pair of double D's that, I must confess, caused quite the pious stir amongst the congregation's brethren.

Oh did the pews creak with the weight of discomfort, and the air fell heavy with the brothers' leery glances and head nods. As their eyes attempted to scan scripture for a footnote on how to handle this unexpected guest with their heart hesitating at the threshold of God's boundless love.

But, ah! Cue the entrance of Brother Gerald, wise as Solomon and steady as Job, who declared with a voice that cut through uncertainty like a hot knife through butter: "In God's house, there are no big I's or small 'me's, just 'we's in the family portrait of the Most High!"
And lo, the clouds of trepidation parted, and the sunshine of acceptance did beam down upon Diamond, who was made to feel as welcome as the Prodigal Son enveloped in the forgiving embrace of his father.

Boy, the message that day was so sharp, the Bible Study transformed right before my eyes into a full-blown, Spirit-led service. Oh yes, by the time Brother Byron took to the pulpit it was as if the ink had just dried. Byron preached on the sacred mathematics of when you seek God first all things will be added unto you. There wasn't a dry eye in the house. Handkerchiefs waved like banners of surrender to the stirring of the Holy Spirit.

Behold, I must say the Spirit moved like a mighty wind through that mosaic of souls. And Diamond, surrounded by the love that had no end and the grace that knew no bounds, shedding tears as a glimmer of hope for the unity in Christ.

Surely as the benediction was pronounced and we parted ways diamond's effulgent personality burst forth. But the seed had been planted, watered by the living waters of sanctuary fellowship.

So let this chapter be a reminder to all. Whether ye be high-stepping in heels or striding in sturdy boots; whether your faith be as a mustard seed or as grand as the cedars of Lebanon; we are all called to the table. And there, in the brilliant humor of life's tapestry, we find our common thread that binds us: the imperative to, above all, put God first.

Remember now, beyond the chimes of the church bell let the echoes of eternal love settle in the chambers of your heart. Amen!

CHAPTER 13 MEETING ON THE MOUNT OF HUMANITY

When we ponder the threads of our Christian faith, woven with holy angelic grace combined in human struggle, we find the intriguing narrative of Jesus Christ meeting people where they are. As ministers of the Gospel, our calling mirrors that of Christ--to descend from our place of comfort, to the valleys of human need by extending a helping hand or a word that uplifts.

For too long walls have been built that separate us, when our gospel-- A gospel of inclusion is about tearing down dividers and building bridges of optimism.

Consider the instant Jesus parted from the heights of the Mount of Olives. The place where heaven seemed to touch the earth. He stepped down not merely in altitude but in the posture of His heart. Moving toward those whose lives were swamped in murky grounds of complexities... you know them they are all around....those who society has often shunned. In like manner, we must also step down from the mount of our own assumptions, descend the slopes of our prejudices and meet each one on their level ground--this ground of our shared humanity.

Take for instance, transgenders on their path to Christ. It's a road often marked by misunderstanding and isolation. As followers of Jesus, we are invited to emulate His example, to come alongside each person on their unique path of faith. Just as Christ called out to Zacchaeus, the tax collector perched in a sycamore tree, when he heard Jesus was coming. Jesus said "Come Down". We must likewise invite the transgenders to share in the fellowship of believers. We must be open to their experiences and listen.

Jesus' ministry was suffused with encounters that crossed cultural and societal boundaries. He dined with sinners, spoke with the Samaritan woman at the well, and offered healing to the Roman centurion's servant. Through these interactions Jesus taught us the radical act of loving beyond convention. When we, as His emissaries, step off our figurative mountaintops and reach out to those who are trans, we are not just ministering--we are loving as He loved. We are acknowledging that they, too, are an integral part of God's family, with gifts and stories that enrich our collective faith journey.

For some time, indeed, we must embody Jesus' willingness to meet people where they are, just

as he met us where we were in our mess. There,
in the depths of our condition, He did not stand
aloof. Here this... to our transgender siblings,
often times marginalized and pushed to the outskirts
of religious communities, we must extend
the same grace that Christ has lavished upon us.
This is not merely a nicety; it is a scriptural
imperative--a manifestation of the love that
covers a multitude of sins.

As ministers of the living Gospel, let us hold
firmly to the promise that, when we meet people
where they are without judgment or hesitation,
we become the vessels of His transformative love.
From this place of heavenly encounter, we do not
merely pull others up--we climb together, side
by side, to the mountaintops of redemption where
every tear is wiped away and every life is
cherished in its glorious reflection of the *41,*
Creator.

So let us go forth in the spirit of Jesus,
to meet others where they stand. Let us affirm
that their journey is sacred, their struggles
are our concerns and their upliftment is our joy.
In this way we bring His healing touch to every
soul Be Blessed!

CHAPTER 14 THE OLIVE BRANCH
"HOSANNA"

In the sacred corridors of scripture, we find a pathway illuminated by the burning love and transformative power of Jesus Christ. As we navigate through the complex tapestry of sexual identity and faith, we must anchor our reflection, in a spiritual truth that is as bound to love as it is to liberty.

When the Apostle Paul addressed the Corinthian congregation I discovered a profound methodology in First Cor. 9:22-23: he says "to the weak I became weak, that I might gain the weak. I am made all things to all men that I might by all means save some. And I do all for the gospel's sake, that I may partake thereof with you." These words resonate with the ethos of 'Transgender Christianity,' which endeavors to reconcile faith with the experience of transgender and gender diverse individuals, as well as those in the greater LGBTQI± community.

In this shared journey of faith, we must become ambassadors of Christ's love, following in the apostolic footsteps to bridge the gap between ecclesiastical doctrine and lived experiences.

Paul's model of ministry challenges us to engage with empathy, to resonate with the beat of another's heart, extending the grace so freely given by our Lord Jesus Christ to all, regardless of gender identity or sexual orientation. Let us examine what it means to be "all things to men" in a broad context to include all genders. Paul was not weak but he became weak to approach each individual he encountered from a place of understanding, compassion and shared humanity. We the church are called to follow Paul's lead becoming a reflection in the water to those who feel unseen or unheard.

We Paul speaks of becoming weak to gain the weak he is encouraging us to lower ourselves, not in stature but in spirit to be able to meet others right where they are in their moments of vulnerability.

Becoming all things does not imply losing our identity or surrendering our convictions rather it means expanding our capacity for understanding and our willingness to walk beside those whose life experiences may differ from our own. It means listening, learning and loving in such a way that we connect bridges of hope and channels of grace.

The gospel is the greater equalizer for the downtrodden it does not discriminate. In the vein of this book 'Transgender Christianity' it is the very lifeblood of salvation that recognizes the intrinsic value of every soul.

When we, I say we because the Holy Spirit was hands on articulating, formulating, editing, etc; Anyway when we dedicate a message in this book we're making a covenant of love that our churches, our ministries and our hearts will be havens of peace. We affirm that the pursuit of saving souls surpasses any barrier. We stand as called servants to serve the least of these with the full measure of compassion.

Our dedication is not only a promise but a proclamation-a call for the Christian community to open its doors wider and let the love of God pour forth onto every individual, affirming their dignity and worth in the eyes of the Creator.

To be partakers of the Gospel is to be partakers in the divine act of redemption. Just as Christ saw fit to walk amongst us in flesh and blood, experiences the full spectrum of human emotion and tribulation, so too must we stand in solidarity with our seekers. For in their lives is the possibility for sanctification and salvation. This book was needed to acknowledge the deep yearning for reconciliation for so many that have fallen away, not just of identities but of soul to Savior. It challenges us to look beyond preconceptions and prejudices to see each individual as Christ sees them-- a beloved child of God, worthy of love, acceptance and eternal life.

Therefore, the charge is ours to carry the Gospel forth with courage, boldness and unwavering love that transcends every boundary, including those of gender. So let this chapter not end of the final words of a page but let it be lived out in your daily actions, relationships, ministry and in general. May we be colaborers in the vineyard, hand in hand with every child of God working together for the sake of the Gospel. Amen!

CHAPTER 15 EMBRACED UNDER THE UNSTAINED GLASS

Child of God, understand that the foundation of your spiritual journey is neither built brick by brick by man's hands, nor hewn from the wisdom of earthly scholars. Rather, it is a divine architecture, a revelation that comes from above, from the whisper and breath of the Almighty Himself. Galatians 1:11-12 declares with emphatic clarity a message not caged by the doctrines of men but released by the revelation of Jesus Christ.

This is foundational teaching of what it means to walk in the liberty wherewith Christ has made us free. Note: The Gospel of Grace, divorced the Law of Moses. Grace must be seen as a canopy that shields us from the rain of condemnation. Once you step under this canopy-- you who once stood out in the downpour of ordinances and statutes "you" can now discern the subtexts of sermons laced with bondage.

There are preachers who hoist homosexuality upon the pike of scrutiny, cherry picking from the Law to reinforce prejudice. Yet, with an artful dodge, the pirouette to the table spread with pork chops and bacon, their lips dripping for a feast.

They forget Christ's teaching that it is not what enters the belly that defiles a man but what emanates from the depths of his heart. Clearly, abolishing the Law on pork and every regulation under it!

We must ask ourselves, what is a spirit of consistency if not a fruit of the Spirit? How do we reconcile the patchwork usage of ancient decrees, summoning them like specters to haunt select narratives while cloaking ourselves in New Testament liberation when appetite dictates?

This selective recollection, this buffet-style theology that stuffs itself on grace with one hand while flinging the law on the other hand, is, a dietary disaster that starves the soul. It's a dual-mindedness that James warns against and it is a direct route to the fall from grace as mentioned in Galatians 5:4 "Christ is become of I no effect unto you, whosoever of you are justified by the law; ye are fallen from grace."

I tell you today, falling from grace is not an accident of misstep or blunder into transgression;, it is a willful step backward into the chains from which Christ has emancipated you. You do not become justified by retracing your steps to Old Testament Mount Sinai (stranded) when you should be advancing towards Calvary and the empty tomb

Beloved, take a minute and look upon the Cross, Jesus cross, the emblem of suffering and shame, and see Christ standing in your place about to be crucified.

Jesus did not bear that ole rugged cross for you to grovel in the dust of guilt when preachers preach condemnation like a cudgel. **Jesus'** blood was not spilled to be temporary balm but a permanent cleansing of the conscience. No, none, notta accusation should hold you captive, no insidious reminder of past failures should shackle your feet when you covered in Jesus' blood.

Being born again, oh beloved, is an unfolding process, akin to an infant learning to navigate the perimeters of a new world--bumps and bruises are to be expected. But remember this it is Christ that will correct you. Not with the intent to punish but to guide, to lead you into the full stature of a child of God. And yes it is true we were all made by Him but becoming children of God is a heritage of faith not of flesh; of Spirit. Not of stones etched with antique commandments. That law was only a schoolmaster, a tutor in our infancy but faith in Christ matured us weigh beyond the classroom of statutes.

Respectfully, the illustrious Apostle Paul was a master in conveying this shift from the Law to Grace. The Promise once confined to the lineage of Abraham secured behind the walls of ordinances is not unleashed to all who would believe by fait The Abrahamic covenant, a silhouette of the New, finds its fulfillment in Christ Jesus who became the Progenitor of a new lineage-- a lineage not linked in the annals of genealogies but written in the Lamb's Book of Life. This is the crux of the New Testament message: it is an echo of freedom, a chorus swelling with the harmonies of Grace.

So, stand fast, therefore, in the freedom wherewith Christ has made us free and be not again entangled with the yoke of bondage. Your covenant with God, sealed by the Blood of his Son, cannot be annulled by any man's condemnation You walk <u>not</u> by the overshadowing of Sinai **but** by the liberating light of Zion's hill. Hold ye head up high in this glorious freedom for it was bought at great price.

Shake off every yoke, reject every whisper of condemnation and let no one deceive you into bartering your freedom for the weak and beggarly elements of the world. You are called to be free and it is in that freedom that you truly serve one another in love. As Galatians 5:13 proclaims "For, brethren, ye have been called unto liberty The message you carry must therefore rise like an incense of grace, flavored with the savory spices of truth. Let your words be seasoned, and your conversations reflect the character of your Father, who loves indiscriminately and whose arms are always open. Remember, it is not the strict adherence to the letter that enlivens but the Spirit who gives life.

In your journey, dear child of God, may you find yourself walking ever closer with Him, adorned in the beauty of Christ's righteousness and enveloped in the infinite grace of the God who calls you his own. For in Christ, we are a new creation, heirs according to the Promise-- children of Abraham by faith and partakers of an eternal unshakable kingdom. **Amen**!

CHAPTER 16 CHRIST COMMANDS NOT COMMANDMENTS

In the gospels, we are given a profound glimpse into the heart of Jesus Christ, who speaks life into the weary and binds up the brokenhearted with words of hope and restoration. His commands are not merely edicts etched in stone but are living, breathing manifestations of love and grace. Beloved, we must grasp this truth, or it underpins the message of the New Covenant that Jesus came to usher in. A bond that transcends the old commandments.

Ponder this, distinct from the directives of the 10 Commandments typical of the Mosaic Law. Jesus declared " A new command I give you: Love one another. As I have loved you, so you must love one another." The rich precept cuts to the very core of our faith, to love extravagantly and without condition, as He first loved us.

Here it is: the Ten Commandments, while vital and foundational, represent God's threshold for human conduct in a fallen world. They set the parameters, teaching us the fundamental rights from wrongs. They are timeless in their wisdom, echoing into the chambers of our conscience. But when Jesus our Blessed Redeemer, stepped onto the scene he fulfills the law and elevated our understanding. He brings the law to life giving it flesh and bones, incarnated it in his being.

When Jesus speaks it is more than a mandate; it
is a transformation -- an intimate rendezvous
from his heart. His voice signals his heartbeat
resonating with divine love, compassion and
inclusivity. Every command of Christ is coated
with the fluidity of grace, stretching to meet us
where we are. Pulling us from the depths of
judgment and ushering us into the light of His
unconditional love.

Seekers I say this: Jesus' command to love
includes "you". You are an integral part of this
Holy Plan woven with the vibrant threads of your
experiences, your pain, your joys and your new
voyage towards walking in the spirit and in truth.
In Jesus eyes, you are precious. Your identity
does not overshadow His command that you are to
be loved too.

Christ commands are the keys to true liberation
and joy. They are not the heavy yokes of legalism
but gentle guidance of a Shepherd leading His
sheep to green pastures and still waters. The
Spirit characterized by justice, mercy and
faithfulness.

In the following commands of Jesus we are tasked with a mission to be light bearers in a world that can sometime be clouded by misunderstanding and fear. Our love is to be radical, reaching across divides and embracing those society has pushed to the margins. It is in the act of loving unreservedly that we reflect the heart of Christ and become true disciples. The call to love is a high calling, demanding all of us.

So, what does this mean practically? It means when we encounter a command from our Savior, we are to discern it not with the lens of the Old but through the eyes of the New--you know the eyes transformed by grace. So hold tightly to the truth that you are included in the cusp of the Almighty that you too are called to love and to be loved for this is the grand commandment of our Lord. Let us go forth being agents of change. Testifying to the power of Christ's inclusive love for all humanity.

CHAPTER 17 SPIRITUALLY NURTURING
THE TENDER BABES IN CHRIST

In the great family of faith, we find ourselves amidst siblings of diverse backgrounds, experiences and stages in their spiritual journey. Like a garden with seedlings and seasoned trees. The body of Christ thrives in its variety and unity. However, some within our fold have very tender shoots of faith, we refer to them as "Babes in Christ" and their spiritual maturity might not correspond to their physical age. They are the nascent believers, sometimes fragile in their understanding and easily overwhelmed--particularly those who identify as carnal, a group for whom the church deemed unwelcome.

In this chapter we consider the necessity of patience, sensitivity, and discretion when guiding baby Christians who are new or struggling in their spiritual walk. Their situation is doubly delicate grappling not only with the novelties of faith but for some their faith has withered.

Language the way we convey communicate and correct carries power to heal or harm it is akin to whispering a lullaby to a newborn: the voice must be gentle; the words nurturing and intentions clear.

Thoughtless remarks or harsh corrections can like a shrill noise cause a spiritual startle-- a breaking of the tender strands of trust that bonded them to Jesus.

Remember Grace is the language in God's Kingdom and every interaction with a spiritual infant should be seasoned with it. Before speaking on matters of correction or discipline prayerfully consider the words to be shared. A spirit-led conversation will reflect Jesus grace no matter. what spiritual circumstance the babe is in. Fostering growth involves highlighting strength not just addressing weaknesses. Always affirm the spiritual strides a babe in Christ has taken will encourage their journey instead of tearing them down. No matter how minor use their framework for teaching.

Now elder infants require measured care that is tailored with precision care and only use it when necessary. Their correction must be applied like a surgeon's scalpel so that they remain in the fellowship.

When it comes to matters of doctrine or church disciple the mentor must distinguish between foundational truths and secondary doctrines. Prioritize patience and understanding over rapid transformation. Offer guidance without overwhelming and use questioning to promote reflection rather than dictating a list of do's and don'ts. Remember babes in Christ are in a process of seeking reconciliation between their identity and their spirituality. Be a source of love and support during this journey. Listen with empathy, acknowledging their struggles.

Spiritual infancy, coupled with the complex path to faith can lead to isolation. Thats why the role of the church is to embrace, include and nurture without judgment. A break in fellowship over misunderstood words or actions is indicative of a need that must be lovingly met.

Sometimes we have to create environments of openness and belonging where Babes in Christ can ask questions without fear and then we can explore their spiritual paths fully supported.

We must emphasize unity of Christ's body, teaching that every member, irrespective of their struggle or spiritual maturity plays a vital role.

Let us remember that our foremost calling is to emulate Christ's love resonating acceptance and patience that allow all children of God to flourish with his divine tapestry.

A WORD FROM THE AUTHORS HEART

During this journey I have encountered the full spectrum of human experience. Trials and triumphs have laid bare before my eyes. And as a caretaker of the Gospel an author who's etched every victory and wrestled with every strife. Has overcome that adversary, crafty and cunning. He doesn't just lurk in the shadows awaiting for a chance to pounce; No he manifests in multifaceted ways, exacting his toll on unsuspecting souls. He preys on the unwary, injecting confusion, doubt and a subtle venom that erodes our understanding of Christ and the sacred mission with which we've been entrusted.

Don't be mistaken by the whispered lies that suggest your faith is a private affair without the need for communion. This is the Spirit of Individualism that feast on isolation.

Breathing illusions into your conscience, seducing you with the notion that you are complete by yourself. Because this very spirit wants to lead you astray, sever you, from the vine--the church "the embodiment of Christ on earth and you my dear child of God are no, irreplaceable fiber."

Do not succumb to this mirage that try to convince you "you" don't need the church. It is not about need; its about purpose. The church, my friends, indeed needs you. Your gifts, your voices, your presence are all integral.

So, I beseech you to fellowship. In times of triumph recall the prayers that lifted you. When surrounded by tempests, envision the sanctuary that awaits. Let not the Spirit of Individualism cast a shadow over the revelation of Christ. The church is not simply a building with four walls and a steeple; it is the collective heartbeat of all who call upon his name. A fortress against the storm and a family bound by the blood shed on Calvary. Yes, the church is your home, and you my beloved are its heartbeat. Be Blessed!

CHAPTER 18 THE GOSPEL UNVEILED

In the heart of the gospel there lies a fervent truth that surpasses all understanding. A truth that embodies unconditional love, infinite grace, and divine invitation for all of God's children. It is in this vivid space that we must open our hearts to recognize everyone is an integral part of the Christian weave. As a Shepherd of His flock, inspired by the ministry and the message of Christ I wish to extend a hand of fellowship and delve into the richness of the gospel that calls us to love without barriers.

This gospel my friends is the good news of Jesus Christ. It speaks to His life, death and resurrection and His ascension. But beyond these historical events the Gospel reveals the depth of God's love for us. It tells a story of redemption and renewal. A narrative in which each of us irrespective of our expression is invited to participate. As it is written "For God so loved the world that he gave his only begotten son that whosoever believeth in him should not perish but , have everlasting life" John 3:16 KJV

The message of Jesus was a radical departure from the exclusionary practices during his time.

Jesus exemplified a path of radial love, where none were turned away. This is the heartbeat of the Gospel. No condemnation but Salvation No rejection but acceptance. No judgment but mercy.

Dear Ones as we reflect on this aspect of Christianity let us not lose sight of its core. LOVE. For all the law is fulfilled in one word. Galatians 5:14 ..Thou shall love thy neighbor as thyself KJV This mandate transcends all else compelling us to look beyond our prejudices and our understandings.

As followers of Christ we are entrusted with the ministry of reconciliation - the calling to bridge divides and heal wounds. I urge you to Stand Firm in the truth of the Gospel that proclaims freedom for the captives and liberation for the oppressed. Let us not add to the burdens the ones struggling carry but let us be the carriers. Let's journey together with them firm in the promise that there is neither Jew nor Greek there is neither slave nor free, there is neither male nor female for we are all one in Christ Jesus.

Thus, let us come together with open hearts and open arms embracing the breadth of God's creation. Let's walk in the footsteps of our Savior who tore down the walls of separation

and built bridges of compassion. Let us be the purveyors of the true Gospel - the good news that proclaims love, asserts dignity and affirms the divine spark within every human being.
In the mighty and matchless name of Jesus may we commit to being a church that embodies the Gospel and be a testament of God's infinite grace for every walk of life. Amen!

CHAPTER 19 GRACE FILLED WITH PLEASURE

Pleasure, a sacred flame, that is as unique as the fingerprints that grace our hands. Just as God whispered to Paul "My grace is sufficient for thee; for my strength is made perfect in weakness.

We too must recognize the incomparable sufficiency of God's grace amidst our personal struggles and delights. We stand today, each of us sculpted elegantly by the infinite wisdom and love of our Almighty God. But what do we mean when we refer to pleasure? Pleasure is the innate tendency within every living being will seek pleasure and avoid pain. It is a guiding light that leads us toward experiences that enrich our souls. It is God's canvas on which He paints the desires and joys that give color to our lives.

Yet, let us not misunderstand dear children of God for this pleasure is not a call to promiscuity nor an invitation to indulge in worldly excess. Rather it is a gentle reminder that within the boundaries of God's love and wisdom there is a space for each human being to experience joy;

Consider the Apostle Paul, the visible form of steadfast faith, who faced trial and tribulations with a "thorn in his flesh".

Paul wanted God to remove the symbolic thorn. And God in his infinite mercy and understanding responded not with the removal of the thorn but with the affirmation of His all-sufficient grace. This exchange between the Divine and His servant is a testament to the reality that our journeys will be filled with challenges that stimulate growth, paired with the recognition that is through God's grace, not the absence of discomfort that we find our fullest expression of life.

In this present age? Many within our ranks have found themselves contending with a society that oftentimes resists understanding the complex narrative of pleasure. Yet, emboldened by the truth of God's all-encompassing love and under the banner of Grace we shall keep journeying. For we know that the Lord does not shun the pleasure principle inherent in His children.

God's grace reminds us that our differences including the myriad ways in which we experience and express pleasure. So, I say this your pleasure, the joy you find in being your truest self, is no accident. It is God's hand at work in your life inviting you to savor your existence.

No matter how society may wrestle with understanding your journey remember that the Creator understands you perfectly, for He is the one who lovingly crafted every difference of your being.

Therefore, let us stride together arms locked hearts open to create a space where every soul can bask in the pleasure of God's creation, unashamed and liberated. For when we stand under the umbrella of God's love we find shelter from the storms of judgment and a refuge for our uniquely individual joys.

In conclusion, when the path seems riddled with thorns, remember that God's grace is a balm, soothing our afflictions and amplifying our delights. It is in this heavenly grace that we are called to live, to love and to find pleasure each according to the marvelous workmanship of our Lord.

May we hold fast to the truth that our individual pleasure is a testament to the vastness of His grace. And let us sing triumphantly with Paul and all the saints. In Jesus Name Amen!

CHAPTER 20 EXPLORING THE SOUL SPIRIT AND FLESH

As we delve into this sensitive topic lets discuss the concepts of the soul, spirit and the flesh which has been the subject of deep theological discourse.

The soul is the seat of emotions and personality. The spirit is the breath of God within us, our essential life force and connection with the divine. The flesh is the physical and carnal nature of humanity for good acts and bad. This chapter seeks to foster a comprehensive understanding of how the soul, spirit and flesh are perceived, manifested and reconciled within this unique context.

In Christianity the soul is paramount. It is the inner essence, the truest expression of identity that often transcends the physical form. The soul houses our feelings, desires and intellect. The soul is a fortified place of truth where the recognition of one's identity resides. Unlike the flesh which may not reflect the individual's inner reality. The soul harbors no such discrepancy, it is the core of personal authenticity. It is critical to understand that within the soul's realm the internal struggle towards self-acceptance for seekers can be incredibly intense.

The soul does not dominate or lead but rather follow the regenerated spirit in a harmonious balance under the guidance of the Holy Spirit. However, when the soul is aligned with divine love and self-recognition the soul emanates peace to live a life of integrity and spiritual wholeness.

The spirit aspect is the divine spark and vertical dimension of our existence that connects us to God. The Spirit is where the intimate relationship with the Creator flourishes, irrespective of fitting or societal acceptance. The spirit is the domain of faith, worship and the relentless pursuit of divine purpose. The engagement with the spirit is pivotal. It is where to seek solace, strength and affirmation from God, who, in his infinite wisdom has created a diverse of human experiences.

We must nurture the spirit through prayer, study and a church community that allows people to transcend. Elevating the believer to a place of divine communion and purpose. The spirit represents the God-conscious part of your being. Now the flesh, that ole fickle unpredictable living creature refers not only to the physical body but also to a way of life that is in opposition to God's Spirit.

The concept of the flesh often presents a dichotomy (division into two parts). When examined from a Christian perspective even though the flesh can lead to sin by carnal desires it is also still the temple or the Holy Spirit.

Let's examine this controversial topic. Very complex in nature that deals with sex changes. Can Christ still be accepted? Here's the complex version- the flesh here may be in disagreement with the soul's truth resulting in a constant battle with one's soul and spiritual identity. This physical appearance includes hormone therapy, gender-confirming surgery, the adoption of a name and/or pronoun that reflects one's soul identity. Through these transformative steps the sex change can accept Christ and experience a harmonization of soul, spirit and flesh, in agreeance with each other. Complex personal choice and free will epitomizing the concept of the temple as wholeness for that person. May God Bless You!

CHAPTER 21 GRACE

I'm going to pose this question: Should my family come to me each bearing a different story, a unique journey one nephew who identifies as heterosexual and one who identifies as trans. Should I embrace them both. Let my arms be a metaphor as the church's embrace, allowing for the love to flow? Or should I deny one and accept the other?

Do not misconstrue my words as an aversion to the shaping of lives in accordance with biblical teachings. It is out of my love for Christ and His teachings that I offer this perspective. I am uncompromising in my belief that we are to nourish our children with virtues of love, kindness and respect for one another. Yet even as I uphold scripture I am careful not to tread upon the delicate gardens of individual journeys with heavy boots of doctrine.

For the preaching of the cross is to them that perish foolishness: but unto us which are saved it is the power of God. First Cor. 1:18 KJV. At the heart of this scripture lies the infinite wisdom of our Lord who chooses to work through the paradoxes and perplexities of our existence.

Grace is the unmerited compassionate favor of our Lord. It is the cornerstone upon which our hope rests. The medicine that heals our wounded spirits. Grace is not earned by works nor by adherence to the law; it is a gift as free as the air we breathe, available to all who reach out wit} open hands and hearts.

In my years of ministry, I have learned that grace is more than a theological concept or a Sunday morning sermon; grace is an ever-present promise, a whisper of divine love that says, "You are seen. You are known. You are cherished. Grace is yours.

Many of you have walked paths riddled with doubt and rejection. Society has often set before you a gauntlet of judgments and even well-meaning congregants have sometimes wielded scripture like a sword rather than a plowshare to till the soil of your hearts. But grace, my friends, reaches beyond the confines of human invention. It does not discriminate. It does not belittle or cast aside.

Please hear me when I say the grace of God envelops you in your entirety. It sees the courage with which you align your outer selves with the truth of your innermost being. The Lord's grace recognizes your journey and says, "You too are fearfully and wonderfully made. Despite the

 voices that may exclude or condemn remember the
voice of grace speaks louder calling you blessed
and made in the image of the Almighty.
Grace is applicable and abundant in the children
of God. It is grace that invites you to take
your rightful place at the table of fellowship,
to partake in the body and the blood, to immerse
yourself in the waters of baptism and to rise anew
Consider the life of Jesus Christ, the
orchestrator of inclusion. He who sat with tax
collectors and sinners embodies a grace that knows
no bounds. In his example we see a love that sets
aside human biases and embraces all in the warmth
of divine kinship.

Do not let anyone convince you that your
struggle disqualifies you from the grace of God.
Ephesians 2:8-9 tells us, "For it is by grace you
have been saved, through faith--and this is not
from yourselves it is the gift of God not by works
so that no one can boast for grace is not an
exclusive privilege but a treasure freely given.
To receive this grace you need only to hold
faith in your hearts and reach out to the One who
provides it. Grace will supply you with the
strength to counter misunderstanding with

enlightenment, rejection with love and hostility with peace. It will empower you to live your life in spirit and truth in the fullness of God's glory. To walk in the conviction that you are a divine creation a vessel of His Spirit.
In conclusion, in our vulnerability God's grace is the sanctuary, strength and the herald of our shared humanity. May we all find solace in the arms of grace. In Love and Faith I pray Amen!

CHAPTER 22 HEAVEN'S ECONOMY

Beloved, let me speak to your heart today about the wealth of righteous deeds. As we open the good book to Matthew 6:20 ...treasures in heaven..., let's turn our minds toward the treasures that rust cannot corrupt and thieves cannot break through and steal. This worldly concept of wealth will have you to believe that wealth is your bank account, your portfolios, your vaults etc; But I tell you today there is an economy greater than any on Earth "Heavens Economy" where your true treasure awaits!

This economy in Heaven isn't swayed by market crashes, it isn't devalued by inflation and it certainly isn't subject to the whims and fancies of earthly systems. It is a spiritual account that is credited with every act of kindness, every word of encouragement, every deed done in the name of Jesus. Can I get an Amen?

Do not fret, child of God, when you feel your good deeds go unnoticed. For every cup of water given to the thirsty, every morsel of food provided to the hungry, every moment spent visiting the sick and imprisoned you're making deposits in the Almighty's bank and your wealth is accumulating where it counts the most. In

Heaven the currency is not gold or silver it is the fruit of your righteous actions, the love you've poured out to others, the compassion you've shown to those in need.

Some of you may say, "I've been laboring Lord I've been toiling and I don't see my breakthrough" But remember we serve a God who is the CEO of the universe. He sees every sacrifice, recognizes every effort and in His divine ledger he's been keeping account of every spiritual transaction. In his glorious Kingdom, the dividends of your spiritual investments will be beyond measure.

Consider this - Earth, fruit is perishable. But not so in Heaven for in that eternal dwelling the fruit is our deeds and their value never depreciate The heavenly father credits your account for your faithfulness, you adherence to His Word and your unwavering commitment to His cause. You see, in heavens economy what truly enriches us is the love we spread, the peace we foster and the hope we instill. I urge, you today do not grow weary in well doing for in due season Did you hear me? For in due season you will reap a blessed harvest if you don't give up. Every minute spent teaching, preaching, loving and lifting up the name of Jesus its an investment earning interest in realms where rust can do no damage.

Lift your eyes, Church, your portfolio in glory is abounding! Your earthly sacrifice is your spiritual gain. Your pain, your trials, your tribulations are your dividends in disguise. So go forth, people of valor, with the certainty that nothing you do for the Lord is ever in vain. Store up treasures in Heaven's economy and when you cross that Jordan, when you set your feet on streets paved with gold you will find your treasure chest overflowing waiting on you saying "Well done, thou good and faithful servant!"

CHAPTER 23 UPHOLDING THE CHURCH
THROUGH GENEROUS GIVING

In the sanctified halls of our congregations, beneath the steeples that pierce the heavens and within the sacred walls that house the melody of praises, there exists a divine invitation-- an invitation to participate in an act of worship intimately tied to our faith: the offering. The moment when the baskets weave through the aisles and hands extend with sacrificial gifts is not to be overlooked or underestimated, for it is as much a part of our worship as the songs we lift and the prayers we exalt.

Dear believers consider the church. It stands not merely as an edifice of bricks and mortar but as a beacon of hope in a turbulent sea, a lighthouse guiding weary souls back home to God's unwavering love. The church, your church, is a vessel through which the Gospel flows into the parched hearts of seekers. We labor together in this vineyard, and our labor includes keeping this vessel strong and seaworthy. Every shingle on the roof, each note from the choir, every word preached from the pulpit and every hand clasped in prayer is borne out of the collective generosity of its members.

A giving heart is at the core of our walk with Christ. The scriptures remind us "Each one must give as he has decided in his heart, not reluctant or under compulsion for God loves a cheerful giver. As shepherd over this blessed narrative I invite you to step into the flow of God's generosity. By doing so, we become channels of His boundless grace and provision.

Let's breakdown the foundations of this sacred duty and privilege for giving is as much of our spiritual DNA as it is a practical necessity.

First, we offer out of obedience. It is written in Malachi 3:10 (KJV) "Bring ye all the tithes into the storehouse that there may be meat in mine house, and prove me now herewith, saith the Lord of hosts, if I will not open you the windows of heaven and pour you out a blessing, that there shall not be room enough to receive it." God has called us to give unto Him first, to lay at His altar the first fruits of our labor, trusting that He who clothes the lilies and feeds the sparrows will take care of our needs in greater measure than we could ever accomplish on our own.

Second, we offer out of need. The church's role as a refuge, a place of teaching, healing and community, requires practical resources.

It is through our offerings that we ensure the lights remain on to welcome the lost at any hour, that the heat runs to warm bodies and souls who enter, and that the outreach programs can operate to extend Christ's love beyond our four walls. We offer because there is work to be done and that work has a cost one that we collectively shoulder.

Third, we offer out of love. Colossians 3:14 states "And above all these things put on charity which is the bond of perfectness." Love compels us to give. It is love for our Creator, appreciation for His endless grace and compassion towards our brothers and sisters that moves us. Giving generously roots us in the understanding that we are but stewards of the blessings we have been given, and it is our privilege to redistribute these blessings in service and in love.

Generosity is not limited by the size of the gift but is magnified by the condition of the givers heart. Whether your offering is a widow's ' mite or the overflow of a bountiful harvest, it is equally precious in the sight of the Lord when given with pure intentions. Within these sacred transactions between us and God, there is a chemistry of the spirit transforming our humble offerings into treasures laid up in heaven.

Recognize family that giving generously is an act of intimacy with our Heavenly Father --it draws us closer to His heart, aligns our will with His and strengthens the Body of Christ, which is the church. It allows the church to stand tall, arms wide open, as a fortress of faith and a sanctuary of peace in a chaotic world.

As we prepare our hearts for the next offering let it be with the fullness of gratitude, the depth of sincerity and the height of faith, knowing that every penny dropped into the basket is a seed sown into fertile ground, a declaration of our trust in the Lord's provision, and a direct contribution to the Kingdom's work. Let us give as God has given unto us--lavishly, joyfully and without measure.

My beloved, in the sacred moment when we pool our resources to keep the church afloat let us not simply part with our resources but let us invest in the eternal, in the immutable kingdom of our gracious Lord. Let the church rejoice for every giver, for every gift and for the boundless opportunities to display the grandeur of God's kingdom to all whom we serve and shelter. Never forsake the assembly. May God Bless You!

CHAPTER 24 A WHISPER OF FAITH

In the annals of history, celebrated are the mighty, the bold, but what about the unnoticed having etched their achievements upon the unyielding tablets of time. Yest, here, within this divine narrative, we pause to listen carefully to the hushed but potent whisper of a young maiden. Her story embedded in the journey of Naaman the Leper.

You see, my dear readers, there are moments crossroads of divine destiny, where the weakest voices speak the loudest truths, echoing forever in the halls of redemption and transformation. It is here we find a nameless servant girl, plucked from the obscurity of her homeland, serving in a foreign house that reecho with the pain of infirmity and the silent cries for healing.

Picture this scene: Naaman, a commander of great bravery. A man of war, cloaked in the spoil of victories, and yet underneath his armor, a secret struggle festered. His skin, a battleground of affliction--Leprosy, a name synonymous with fear and irreversible decay. In the shadows of this grandeur lurks the gentle spirit of a servant girl, grafted into the narrative by the divine hand of providence. Her life interrupted by captivity but her spirit was flickering with the light of faith. Oh, what a person would do to have the faith of this young girl. She was the servant and in the eyes of man back then women dared to speak especially to a situation destined uncured.

The young girl spoke out anyway to the mistress saying "If only my master would go see the prophet in Samaria! "He would cure him of his leprosy" based on these words alone a cascade of divinity rushed forth, her declaration becoming the crux upon which the story would pivot.

Let us pause and reflect on the magnitude of her words, laden with a faith that transcends her dire circumstances. How easy it would have been for this young girl to just succumb to this bitterness. Just letting her spirit be quenched by the bondage she was enduring. Oh, but the Spirit of the Lord had placed something far grander within her young heart. She did not permit her condition (in shackles) affect her position (in God). Here she is without fanfare or title effectively altering the course of a man's destiny as she raised her voice in a testament of unshakable belief in the power of the Almighty.

What can we glean from this unnoticed heroine of healing. As carriers of Christ we have to speak to the storms of life.

In today's clamorous world recall the good brother Jo Jo our esteemed brother walk in integrity of speech. He is careful, ever so careful, not to speak evil into existence, illustrating a deep understanding that the words we impart can manifest realities both good and bad.

The brother praised so hard at one of the Bible Study's shouting "Hallelujah" it resonated within our whole sanctuary walls. His praise was not just noise; it was powerful, it was purposeful it was prophetic. You could not help but to hear the authority, confidence and clarity that it seemed a mouthpiece strictly made for the Almighty Himself, stirring the spirits of all who l were privileged to hear him. Jo Jo's voice commanded attention--not because of its tonal quality which bore no scratchy baritone or irksome bass, but because his praise was crystal clear, a pure vessel for divine works.

So, we thank Brother Jo Jo cause when he lifts his voice its not just the timbre that captivates(us; it is the Shepherd's voice we discern, a voice marked by love, wisdom and truth. How crucial it is then to use our voices to speak life into a dead situation or give praise in the pitfalls of hell. "Hallelujah!" Let it be the sound that launches a thousand actions, a million missions and countless heartfelt gestures. Just like Brother Jo Jo ...believers with anointed voices SPEAK and let the world hear Jesus through you. AMEN! AMEN! AND AMEN!

CHAPTER 25 THE DIVINE CHECKMATE: A SPIRITUAL HUSTLE IN EXODUS

Now, I was doing my study the other day, turning the delicate pages of the Bible when I was led upon a yarn in Exodus that made me lean back and say "WOW" because it exposed every storm that was coming at me.

This saga of a slave driver by the name of Pharaoh known as the top dog back in Egypt had a hard heart. Not by nothing he did but God did it. Scholars have been scratching their heads, tugging on their beards and sipping on their teas for ages pondering the curious question of Why would God harden Pharaoh's heart?

Why not give Pharaoh a heavenly heart? Make it tender like Sunday morning biscuits? Her-Vs the revelation; Since our God ain't no puppet master we've got free will. He doesn't do remote control. Our God isn't looking to robotize us into holy rolling robots, oh no. He wants us to choose. Make a conscience decision to take one step forward and he will do the rest.

Picture this with that hard heart of Pharaoh when he finally caves in or more like crumble under the weight of God's persuasive techniques of letting Pharaoh witness the Israelites receive favor. What seemed to be a setback is a set up.

So, there I was, Bible in hand, eyebrows raised, trying not to spill my own tea, as the narrative unfolded. God had sent a cadre of plagues upon Egypt, each one like a card up His divine sleeve - boom, boom, boom! What is it now the other people wondered what plague was coming next while our Israelite kin did not even flinch or stub a toe!

Exodus 9:6 lays it out plain as day: "And the Lord did that thing on the morrow, and all the cattle of Egypt died but the cattle of the children of Israel died not one." Here it is they in the same situation but the children of God receiving favor with a capitol "F". Somebody say favor out loud just to speak it into your life. It's like the Master of the Universe has your back with VIP passes to the front row of blessings.

So, lo and behold, no sooner did the Israelites shake the dust off their sandals Pharaoh's heart get turned to stoned again. The Red Sea had already opened and the Israelites had crossed it on dry land then here come Pharaoh and his posse come rumbling down the sea--chariots a-blazin. The scene looked like a chariot chasing sea splashing spectacle! You could see Pharaoh huffing and puffing hankering for a grand showdown by the Red Sea. The Israelites had barely got their toes wet getting ready to enjoy their new life. God had to quickly pull a Houdini on Pharaoh and his henchmen. Pharaoh did not know he had been set up from the get go. While he was playing checkers God was f playing Chess - Pharoah CHECKMATE God hollered!

GAME OVER! Pharaoh knew the Israelites had a powerful God but never thought when he parted the Red Sea and let his children pass through God -would fill the Red Sea back up with all Pharaoh and his henchmen inside the sea. Pharaoh and all his men died by drowning. Was that spiritually gangsta? God putting the 'G' in Glory moving with purpose and finesse. Or just an accident?

No, take this tale from the book of Exodus, weave it into your spirit and remember: when life throws plagues your way, when the Pharaohs of your storm keep knocking. Pause a minute, take a breath and know that the Lord's favor is fierce and his game plan is unfathomable. You might feel like you're up against a Red Sea with nowhere to turn, but baby, that's just a setup for your breakthrough. Hold tight, step forth in faith for your Divine Deliverer always has an exit strategy that'll leave you in awe. And with God' sense of humor, you'll find yourself walking on dry land shouting "thanks for favor" for all the heavenly host to rejoice with ya. Can I get an "Amen"? May blessing continue to chase you down GOD BLESS.

CHAPTER 26 THE EVERLASTING MERCY SEAT

In Hebrews 9:12 we hear the echo of ancient truth, whispering through time, all the way from the shadows of the Old Testament rituals to the breaking light of the New Covenant. It explains back then "Neither by the blood of goats and calves, but by his own blood he entered in once into the holy place, having obtained eternal redemption for us."

Let's take a break to dissect this mercy seat through the lens of grace. For it is at the mercy seat where the very essence of our faith rests. It's at the mercy seat, beloved, where every chain is broken and every boundary is overshadowed by grace. It's where Jesus, our High Priest, did not just sprinkle animal blood as was the custom but he presented his own blood. Oh, how majestic! Ensuring that even when the death angel comes, it has to pass over, cause we are covered in a blood weigh more potent and everlasting than any annual sacrifice of old.

This mercy seat detailed in the Old Testament was the lid atop the Ark of the Covenant residing in the inner sanctum of the temple, the Holy of Holies. It was here, once a year, that the high priest would enter with trepidation, bearing sacrificial blood to atone for the people's sins. What's going on here is the transcendence of that Old Covenant. Not in a temple made by hands but a direct line into the very throne room where Jesus ! carries our redemption.

When we meditate on Jesus crucifixion we can understand how he is both the High Priest and the, Lamb. Christ just didn't bring the blood to the altar he was the altar. He just didn't provide the sacrifice he was the sacrifice. There's no outcast at the mercy seat.

If nothing else, hear this, in Hebrews we are reminded that the rituals of blood are no longer needed for the Mercy Seat has been forever changed through the blood of Jesus. Now all are covered. All are welcomed. No life is unseen in the sight of the Almighty. In spiritual solidarity, we can look towards the Mercy Seat not with fear but with hope. This mercy seat is a reminder Jesus bridged the chasm of separation with nails in his hands and feet and with a crown of thorns upon his brow.

Let us then, with hopeful hearts, with joyous strides, proceed knowing that the blood of Christ is enough. We cannot continue to put Christ back ! on the Cross. Jesus has consecrated a new 1 covenant. Not just one written on stone tablets but upon the very fibers of our being. This mercy seat is where Heaven's justice and compassion waltz in perfect harmony. You my dear are not forgotten or forsaken. Now walk in this blood you are covered with no matter how the world view you be seen as sacred and fitfully redeemed reflection of the Creators grand design BE BLESSSED!

CHAPTER 27 EMBRACE YOUR ROLE AS A STEWARD OF WEALTH

Friends, believers and family, as we journey through this existence, we come to understand our lives through experiences and teachings that we hold dear. Among those teachings, there are principles that challenge our very perception of wealth a topic that can be divisive and misunderstood, but one that also holds the potential for liberation and empowerment within our Christian walk. Money, indeed, is not inherently evil it is the love of it that scripture warns us against.

But I want delve deeper and examine this through the lens of stewardship, particularly within the context from a spiritual standpoint. A path where faith and greed intersect in profound and often times challenging ways.

Consider this: the Earth and everything in I belong to the Lord (Psalm 24:1). That includes the money in your possession. We as believers as individuals who walk in diverse experiences are merely stewards of what God has graced us with. This isn't a new concept its determining I God wants to be an active owner or passive owner This stewardship isn't merely about management its about partnering--with the Holy Spirit in acknowledgment **of** God as the active Owner and Provider, and about aligning our financial decisions with divine wisdom.

Now if you find yourself in the folds of controlling wealth, you are no stranger to the delicate balance of embracing your role, while holding onto your faith. You understand what it means to navigate spaces that don't always speak your language "BOSS TALK" or acknowledge your mission. Money and resources in your hands become not only a tool for survival but a means for advocating tangible expressions of love and justice. But, as with all tools entrusted to us by the Divine the purpose of which we use them should always reflect the heart of our Savior.

Imagine a situation where you're entrusted with millions precious, by someone you deeply respect and love. Would you use it recklessly or thoughtlessly? Most likely, you'd exercise great care and seek to use it in ways that honor the trust placed in you. This is the relationship with God regarding money.

In the community of believers, the need for careful stewardship is pronounced. Resources can be scarce and the stewardship of money become about survival, about creating affirming spaces, and about ensuring that resources are channeled towards where they are needed most. It's not merely about surviving individually; its about thriving together. Remember, within the body of Christ when one part flourishes the whole body flourishes.

Moreover, reflecting on the intersection of faith and money especially under the Christian umbrella one must consider the Holy Spirit's role in our financial decisions. The Holy Spirit is not silent; it moves, it speaks and guides. When it whispers to your heart about generosity or caution against self-indulgence, it's a directive from heaven. It's God's way of saying, 'You are my child, my rep., and my steward in this world.

Therefore, act in a way that furthers the kingdom, Jesus love and Jesus justice. Never quench the spirit when it comes to financial matters. Each penny spent should be a seed sown into the ground of God's Kingdom, each dollar a testament to your trust in God's money on earth. This is not to say that one shouldn't enjoy the fruits of their labor, but rather that joy should never be decoupled from responsibility. For when we spend without heed, we muffle the voice of the Spirit, and we risk stepping into the territory of greed--the very love of money that the scripture warns against.

Now, in embracing this truth of stewardship Christians have a powerful opportunity to set an example. When resources are managed wisely, when money is seen as a tool for God's glory rather

than a private treasure trove, a powerful state
is made. We declare, without speaking, that
our trust is not in wealth, but in the Provider
of all things.

Let's be clear--a steward is not merely an
overseer but a caretaker, a guardian, a custodian
Your experiences, your struggles and victories
in navigating your faith and identity have
uniquely positioned you to understand what it
means to care deeply. Translate this into how you
approach the resources God has placed in your
hands.

But bear in mind, the true wealth in this
stewardship is not the money itself but the
growth, the maturity and the blessings that come
from handling it rightly. For as we align our
financial dealings with God's will,
selves up to the true riches--those of the Spirit.

In closing, let me remind you that through the
journey of Spirituality it can be fraught with
difficulties, it is also replete with opportunities
for God to showcase His all-encompassing„
love through you. You have been called not just
to be recipients of His grace but to be conduits
through you. You have been called not just to
be recipients of His grace but to be conduits
through which that grace can flow into the world.

So let us each examine our hearts, reconsider our stance on money and realign our financial practices with the knowledge that we are caring for God's wealth you have been entrusted to govern with gratitude for the sake of His Kingdom. Praise the Lord!

CHAPTER 28 FORGIVENESS: THE PATH
TO HEARTFELT LIBERATION

In the profound words of our Savior we have often heard, "Forgive us our trespasses, as we forgive those who trespass against us." This is a pillar of the Christian faith, upon which we lean when the storms of life seek to uproot us from the soil of serenity. Yet, in the complexity of our human emotions, particularly when navigating the delicate intricacies of things we don't understand in life forgiveness becomes not merely, a verbal offering but a journey that takes root in the crevices of our hearts.

As a community of faith, we have witnessed the transformative power of forgiveness in order to be forgave. Not just in the abstract but as a concrete bridge from pain to peace, from turmoil to tranquility. However, let us not be misled;: This bridge is not constructed with the frail timbers of empty words. Instead, it is forged with the resilient steel of genuine forgiveness--a forgiveness that is felt before it is spoken, that resonates within before it emanates outward. Individuals within the Christian faith often stand at the intersections of understanding 1/2 the full Gospel. Wondering who, why and how?

Yet, even within our sacred communities, the road to this solace is always marred with potholes of prejudice and the gravel of misunderstanding, often necessitating a level of forgiveness on various levels.

To grasp the full gravity of heartfelt forgiveness,
we must first acknowledge the effort it requires. It is not an act of weakness but of being not easily discouraged or defeated. It does not mean condoning harm or absolving others of their accountability. Instead, it is about freeing oneself from the shackles of harbored hurt and recognizing that holding on to pain only poisons the vessel that contains it.

My beloved, there is a sacredness in forgiveness that echoes through the annals of time, harking back to the moment when Christ, on that rugged cross, forgave those who knew not what I they did. In that divine act of mercy, we find the template for our journey towards authentic forgiveness--the kind that nestles within the soul and sparkles through the eyes.

Heartfelt forgiveness within the Christian Community requires an understanding that the forgiveness journey will be tense with its struggles. It is not necessarily a swift journey but rather one that may require wrestling with our innermost feelings, much like Jacob wrestled with the angel until the breaking of the day.

It requires patience and compassion, not just for others, but for oneself as well.

The process begins with introspection, with turning inward to listen to the hurt, the fears, and the hopes that play the silent hymns of our spirit. There, in that internal sanctum, we begin to understand that forgiveness does not change the past, but it has the power to change the future. It is a choice to let go of the desire for retribution, to rise above our human instinct for recompense, and to walk in the light of a love that covers a multitude of sins.

As Christians journey toward the summit of heartfelt forgiveness, let them be reminded that they are not alone. Within this voyage lies a shared human experience that bonds us, whether we tread the path as allies, advocates or as pilgrims navigating the truth. It is a communal trek, where the burdens of one become lighter when lifted by many.

Healing begins where hurt once resided, and peace plants its roots where turmoil once was sown. It is in this sacred exchange that we learn the art of true forgiveness--not just saying "I forgive," but allowing those words to blossom into actions and attitudes, permeating the very essence of our being.

There is a transformative beauty in forgiveness that transcends human understanding, one that must be pursued with relentless devotion. For us Christians, this means walking the path laid out by the One who has forgiven us, encouraging us to extend that same grace to ourselves and to those around us.

This heartfelt forgiveness is not an effortless endeavor; it is a purposeful stride towards I redemption and reconciliation. It is a declaration that we will no longer allow the past to dictate the quality of our present or the promise of our future. It is the ultimate testament of our faith and the undeniable evidence of the Creator's work within us. So, let us embark upon this journey with determination with our hearts wide open to the possibilities that forgiveness presents. And as we do, let us remember that in the act of heartfelt forgiveness, we are not merely uttering words; we are unlocking the doors to our fullest potential in Christ, allowing His love to flow through us uninhibited and pure. GOD BLESS!

CHAPTER 29 A NEW SEASON OF GRANDADS

A granddad at the age of 35? Today we find ourselves in a new period in history of rapid transformation, an actual crossroad between being unworthy of respect and the traditions of yesteryear. Amidst this generational change, there emerges a new archetype that defies the generation of wisdom we've come to expect--these are the Young Granddaddies of Generation X. Men of a certain youthful vigor barely beyond the flush of their own youth being called granddad. Already anointed with the title of a grandfather.

Once upon a time, to be called granddad was to have walked a long road, to have the silver crowns of wisdom glistening upon one's temple, the slow t gait of experience pacing one's stride. It was to I have lived through seasons of trials and triumphs to I have their stories that stretched back through decades, weaving the tapestry of family legacy wit} threads of resilience, sacrifice and an unquestioned authority born of age.

But today, these young granddaddies, they shatter the stained-glass window of the old image. At the tender age of 35, some of them are standing at life's pulpit, already called to the ministry of grandparenthood', while their peers are still tasting the wine of life's early ventures. They sport fashionable garb, their footsteps march to

the rhythm of the latest beats, and their language
is steeped in the parlance of a generation that
refuses to grow old and embrace their title.

We see them nestled in parks, the lines of age
yet to claim their brows their backs unburdened by the
stoop of time. They play with their grandchildren, the
energy undiminished, a mirror of the youth they still
clutch. They share selfies hash tagged moments of a
granddad's life, where the playground of social media
allows them to redefine the role that time has
traditionally carved. No more board games of old way.
Everything is digitized. And yet, beneath this veneer
of prolonged youthfulness, we must pause and consider
what it truly means. There lies a potential pitfall
in embracing grandparenthood without the profundity
of maturity. The gift of legacy is not merely in
the biological link of lineage but in the spiritual
and emotional wisdom that is passed down through
the years.

Immaturity, adorned in the garb of a grandparent,
risk diluting the holiness of that role.
Why not preach to these youth. Plant seeds of
Jesus through prayer. The young granddad must
therefore rise to the occasion, to embrace not
just the title but the responsibility that comes
with it. It means being a beacon when the family
sea turns rough demonstrate faith. For these
young granddaddies, it is a divine calling
to redefine what grandparenthood means in this
new age. These young patriarchs rewrite the scrip

Let them wear their youth like a badge of honor but let them not forget that they are the roots of tomorrow's trees tasked with the solemn duty of providing shade and sustenance to the saplings that spring forth from their lineage of faith.

As the world watches let this moment in history be your calling to stand tall, to grow wise, and 1 to lead with the kind of love and strength that will make your grandchildren look back, years hence, and say with pride "My granddad was a fountain of youth but his heart was an ancient well of wisdom. May God Bless You!

CHAPTER 30 THE VITAL CALL TO FELLOWSHIP AND THE BREAKING OF STRONGHOLDS

Beloved open your heart to the revelation bestowed upon us by the Divine. I want you to surf with me through the scriptures, to a passage that speaks to the core of our deliverance, hidden within the book of Isaiah: "And it shall come to pass in that day, that his burden shall be taken away from off thy shoulder, and his yoke from off thy neck and the yoke shall be destroyed because of the anointing." Isaiah 10:27 KJV only.

This powerful verse served as a testament to the strength that is found in the unity of the Body of Christ. It is in the physical house of God my dear family, that yokes are broken and burdens are lifted. There's something miraculous about being in the very presence in the sanctuary God has appointed for us to convene.

Now I understand the convenience and the comfort that can come from virtual worship especially in a time where technology has enabled, us to connect across vast distances. It has been' a blessing for many, particularly in times of great trial. But let us not mistake this supplement for the sustenance that only comes when we gather with our full selves - mind, body and spirit within the consecrated walls of the church.

Virtual worship, while valuable in certain aspects, is somewhat akin to nourishing our bodies on bread alone when our souls are yearning for the meat of fellowship. It is in collective worship that we feel the heartbeat of the vibrantly in motion beating to the tune of harmony and faith in all Jesus has done. The true church is there particularly in times of great trial. But let us not mistake this communal anointing that the binding of us standing together cause strongholds pain and fear to fall away when we stand united in Christ love.

I urge you, do not forsake the assembly Hebrews 10:25. Virtual worship in this digital age may seem convenient, but it can inadvertently become a yoke that keeps us isolated - the very opposite of the way to which we are called as members of the body of Christ. Our coming together is not just a mere formality, it is the fulfillment of Christ's vision for His Church, the embodiment of His love manifested through our fellowship.

The environment of the church, the physical gathering of believers, is a place where strongholds are shattered. There is a tangible manifestation of the Holy Spirit's power as we lift our voices in unison, praising the One who gave all so that we might live free. In the synergy of worship and in the handshaking of peace strongholds lose their grip when the energy of the church flows fluently.

\

Family, you are part of this body. You are called by God, and his desire is for you to experience the full measure of His love among your' fellow believers. The journey can be difficult, and the road can feel lonely, but within the communion of saints and the ministry of the church: you will find strength and power to overcome every yoke that seeks to bind you.

So come, come into His presence with thanksgiving,
gather in His sanctuary, and allow the healing ointment of fellowship to soothe your soul. For it is here, in the sacred embrace of the living body of Christ, where true freedom is found and strongholds are broken by the powerful anointing of His unstoppable grace. Come back home **to the church and pull down your** blessings! AMEN! AMEN! and AMEN!

CHAPTER 31 THE UNFORGIVABLE ACT

In the midst of a world brimming with diversities of doctrines and theologies there sprawls an immutable truth that towers over the landscape of Christian belief, unshaken and unchangeable-- blasphemy against the Holy Spirit remains the singular unpardonable sin. Mark 3:29 warns with a clarity that pierces the soul, "He that shall blaspheme against the Holy Ghost hath never forgiveness but is in danger of eternal damnation.

The gravity of this scripture can turn the heart cold and push the spirit into a state of contemplation, for it speaks of a boundary set by God, a righteous deity who is far from the arbiter of arbitrary decrees. No, this commandment is anchored in the grand canon of divine love and an ocean of a holy and just relationship between Creator and creation.

To speak against the Father, against the Son and against the Holy spirit is not merely an offense against an abstract concept; it is a transgression against the foundational essence of God's being and the cornerstone of our faith. These three are one. The Holy Trinity is the representation of God's complete and perfect unity, a harmony that defines the very nature o God's interaction with humanity. To utter blasphemies against this perfect unity is to reject God in His fullness.

The Father, the architect of existence, the author of our beginning and the promise of our future; the Son, the incarnate Word, the bridge between divinity and humanity, the embodiment of salvation; and the Holy Spirit, the quiet whisper of the roaring wind, the comforter and advocate operate as 1. To speak unpleasant about any part of this Holy Trinity is to set oneself against the entirety of God's manifest presence.

Consider the setting of Mark 3: the scribes, learned men in knowledge who should have known the divine but made the catastrophic error of attributing the work of the Holy Spirit through Jesus to a fake god Beelzebub as if he did all the works Jesus had did. But think about it how can Satan cast out Satan. This was not an accidental slip of the tongue, not a momentary lapse of judgment; it was a willful, conscious decision to reject the irrefutable evidence of the divine before them. Jesus, in His divine wisdom and grace speaks a sobering truth --that there is a line which when crossed, eliminates the possibility of a return to grace.

Why does such a line exist? Understanding the: character of God reveals that He does not have mood changes or is cruel. Rather, the line represents the critical importance of relation- (ships, acknowledgment and heart posture. To deny the Holy Spirit is to refuse the birthing agent of change, the One who convicts the world,

who corrects the believer, who counsels the back
slider and who comfort the spiritually wounded.
It is a denunciation of the only means by which
our hearts can be transformed and aligned with
God's holy standards.

This text, dear reader, is not provided to
instill fear but to invite introspection. For the
essence of this warning is rooted not in the act
of an accidental utterance but in the condition
of the heart that propels it. God, in His boundless
generosity, has given us free will--the
capacity to love, to reject, to choose. When
someone blasphemes against the Holy Spirit, they
exercise this free will in the most tragic of
fashions, for they choose to seal their hearts
against the transformative power of God's love.

Remember, the true nature of blasphemy against!
the Spirit is not found in questions and doubts,
for these are but the stirrings of a seeker's
heart. Nor is it encapsulated in the struggles
and failings that each one of us endures, for we
serve a God lavish in forgiveness and abundant,
in mercy. The unforgivable sin is the persistent
and resolute rejection of the Spirit's witness
to the truth of Jesus Christ--the deliberate step
away from the light back into an eternal darkness,:
a willful wandering from the pathway of salvatio4
cut short speaking against Jesus.

My beloved, this chapter is not to cast you into despair but to awaken you to the reality of our spiritual battlefield. Let us not be like those scribes, blinded by pride or tradition. Let us instead heed the call to a life in step with the Spirit, a life rich with repentance and humility. Our Almighty God has given His Son that we might have life, and in recognizing the Holy Spirit's work, we honor that priceless gift. If you don't have Christ how are your sins forgiven since there are no more sacrifices Christ was the last one. And the curtain has been ripped apart. BE BLESSED!

CHAPTER 32 OBEDIENCE

Obedience in the fabric of our spiritual walk is a hallowed strand that weaves through the very core of our journey--the strand of obedience. This divine principle, reverberated through the annals of scripture and echoed within the sanctum of our hearts, calls us to a posture of submission to the voice of God. It beckons us, ever so gently yet persistently to abide to the whispers of the Holy spirit, no matter how the command may challenge the norms of our understanding or the comforts of our predispositions.

In the subconscious of our mind there lies a ; profound truth. It's the voice of the Holy Spirit that remains a reminder and guide amidst the scene of confusion in moral chaos and the violent whirlpool of societal expectations, especially in the nuances of Christianity where the intersection of faith meets identity. Imagine if you will, a path laid before you, not with the cobblestones of human making but with the interplay of rainbow like colors that glow of the Divine's intention.

This path is illuminated by the gentle yet unyielding light of the Holy Spirit, and along this path, God himself commands us to walk. So what happens when we have to make a decision having heard the voice and yet choose to veer off, into the thicket of rebellion? You see my dear when the Holy Spirit speaks directly to you that is for you that is your command urging you to obey whatever is being revealed.

To unite the words faith and obedience might in itself present a challenge as if since you did not obey you lost your faith? Do we offend God when we are obedient? Do we lose our faith when we are obedient? Yet throughout Scripture we find episodes of disobedience that led to consequences.

In the Garden of Eden, Adam and Eve's disobedience to the divine command fractured the primordial fellowship with God. In the Kingdom of Israel, Saul's inability to adhere to commandments of God, led to his downfall and the rise of David, a man after God's own heart. And let us not forget Jonah his flight from the call to preach repentance to Nineveh landed him in the belly of a great fish. These stories of disobedience mirror the grave consequences of disregarding the voice of God, and they echo a warning for us today.

Christians who hold faith dear grapple with a nuanced type of obedience. For some might question how does one hear the voice of the Holy Spirit when it calls into question the very nature of ones character. The call to obedience in this sphere is not about adhering to an interpretation marked out by societal norms or traditional religious tenets but rather about being true to the personal relationship between you and Christ. Same as if your significant other warns you.

Obedience to the voice of the Holy Spirit is an act of courage that transcends the simple act of listening. It is about the convergence of hearing and acting. It requires us to walk boldly in the direction that God ordains, no matter how unpredictable or daunting the path may appear. It demands a trust that bids us to surrender to His supreme authority and embrace who we have been created to be.

So, when the Holy Spirit speaks and we choose to silence that voice we opt for conformity over God's directive only then do we embody the essence of disobedience. This form of rebellion is not merely a benign act of defiance--it is one that stifles the transformative work of the Spirit: It hinders our testimony, for how can we proclaim , the gospel of love and authenticity if we ourself eschew the very core of our being and the echo of divine truth within us?

Family we must recognize that to disobey the Holy Spirit when He directs us in truth is just like wading in troubled waters. Pretty soon you will not be able to hear that voice it will slowly fade away instead of being loud and clear. For our God is a relational entity, one who desires communion and fellowship with the children He so dearly loves.

To the Christian believer of today, your testimony of obedience is powerful. It serves as a beacon of hope that affirms the truthfulness of the Gospel. Your commitment to the whispers of the Holy Spirit announces to the world that obedience is not a relic of bygone faith but a living testament of God's ongoing work in our life.

In conclusion, obedience to the Holy Spirit is neither trivial nor inconsequential; it is central to our communion with God. It requires attentive listening, unwavering courage and a commitment to action. To heed the voice that speaks to our true self is to honor God and to ignore it is to trespass against His loving desire for our wholeness. Let us, therefore, strive to walk in the path of obedience allowing the Holy Spirit to guide us into the fullness of life and into the glorious reality of being true to ourselves and true to God. This, indeed, is the highest form of worship and an offering most pleasing to the Lord. STAND FIRM

CHAPTER 33 SILENCE IS GOLDEN

In the tapestry of biblical narratives Jesus stands as a figure of absolute composure and wisdom. He was perpetually under intense scrutiny from the religious leader of His time, particular the Pharisees. These religious leaders were not just caretakers of the Hebrew law but were often riddled with hypocrisy and a deep-seated need to maintain their social and religious agendas. Jesus fully aware of their intentions provide us with an example of an impeccable character that is relevant throughout the ages.

The Pharisees often approached Jesus with cunning questions hoping to trap Him in His words They were poised like predators, ready to pounce on any misstep, to twist His words, and to incite! the masses and the Roman authorities to go against Jesus. In the Gospels according to Mark, Luke and: John numerous instances of these kind of confrontations occurred.

Yet, in these encounters, Jesus exemplifies the epitome of one who exercises the discipline of the tongue. In the book of Proverbs, King Solomon speaks to the wisdom of controlling one's, speech: "Whoever guards his mouth and tongue keeps his soul from troubles" Proverbs 21:23. Understanding the gravity of spoken words, Jesus navigated the treacherous waters of social interaction and political intrigue with exemplary skill. He demonstrated an understanding that many today lack: Not every question requires an answer and not every accusation deserves a response. Instead, Jesus chose either to remain silent or to speak with such purposeful clarity that His message would not just resonate but echo throughout history. His silence was not of defeat or timidity; it was a calculated and powerful tool against a backdrop of provocation.

When the high priest questioned Jesus during His trial, as presented in the book of Mark, the Savior knew well that any answer given in that charged atmosphere would have been fuel for the fire of falsehood. He embodied the wisdom of silence, offering no handle for His words to be twisted or His thoughts manipulated. In those moments he remained silent; He communicated a profound message--sometimes strength is not in the words uttered but in the courage to withhold them even when every fiber of one's being cries out for justice or vindication.

However, when He spoke, Jesus was deliberate. He used parables and direct statements, knowing that these words would be carried on the wings of intention to the ears of those ready to receive them. He was not passive in His interactions. When He perceived hypocrisy, He addressed it with such precision that it left the Pharisees, exposed and confounded. We remember how He rebuked them saying, "Woe to you, teachers of the law and Pharisees, you hypocrites!" revealing their inner corruption and cautioning the masses to heed their teachings but not to follow their example Matthew 23:2-3 KJV

Jesus taught us that it's not only about what you say but also how and when you say it. With the Pharisees, He was assertive without being aggressive, profound without being pretentious. He spoke truth to power not with an aim to win every argument but to offer a pathway to transformation and enlightenment.

Dear Reader, consider the depth of self-mastery demonstrated by our Lord. It calls us to a higher standard of interaction, to be beacons of light in a world that offer rewards the clever ones with a witty reply over the thoughtful reply. In a society quick to speak and slow to listen, we are reminded by the Prince of Peace that there is strength in silence and in speech seasoned with grace.

In emulating Christ, we are encouraged to practice restraint, to value the wisdom of silence, and to recognize the potential impact our words can hold. How many disputes could be diffused if we made the conscious choice to hold our tongue? How many relationships could be salvaged if we sought to speak with clarity and compassion rather than with an attitude? As followers of Christ, we are invited to let our communication be a reflection of His

love and wisdom. To have our speech guided by
the principles He embodied and our silence
marked with purpose and intent. The Messiah was
not riveted by the need for approval, nor swayed
by the fear of misunderstanding; He remained
steadfast in truth and love.

In your own life, dear reader, may you find
the courage to harness the power of your words
and the wisdom to know when to let silence speak
volumes. "It's not just about going through life,
but growing through life and becoming all that
God has ordained you to be." Let the way Jesus
controlled His tongue and utilized silence be
a demonstration. For in the echoes of His words
and the quietness of His pauses lies a path for
us all--a path of integrity, of power and of
divine presence amidst the clamor of the world.
God Bless!

CHAPTER 34 YOU NEVER KNOW HOW THE
LORD WILL USE YOU TODAY

My beloved family, we stand today at the crossroads of trials and triumphs, often entangled in a tumultuous battle that seems to lean in favor of the adversary. And yup, in the middle of our despair, when darkness seems to swallow the light of our hope, there comes a word, a scripture, a divine promise that shines through the obscurity: Romans 8:28 declares, "And: we know that all things work together for good to them that love God, to them who are the called according to His purpose."

Let me take you on a journey through the profound depths of this scripture, for it serves, as a balm to our wounded spirits and a fortification for our weary souls. When it feels as though Satan himself is tightening his grip on your 7 circumstances, whispering lies that your situation. is beyond redemption, remember this divine ft c, assurance: you may not see it now, you may not understand it later, but the Lord is at work in your life. You are an instrument in His grand concerto, and He has not forgotten the sheet music of your days.

Often, our human sentiments are besieged by

the notion that success is free from struggle,
that victory comes without battle, that to be
touched by God is to be immune from the wiles of
the enemy. But herein lies a fundamental
misunderstanding of the divine process. For gold to
emerge its finest state, it must encounter fire;
for a diamond to manifest its brilliance, it must
endure pressure. Likewise, for God to mold us
into the vessels fit for His use, we must sometimes
face the furnace.

The Lord, in His infinite wisdom and supreme
craftmanship, does not discard us when we are
tarnished by life's trials; instead, He uses
those very trials as tools for our transformation:
The challenges that you perceive as Satan getting.
the best of you are often the raw materials God
uses to build within you a resilience, a tenacity,
and a faith that no claim seas could ever produce
Do not despise your struggle, for within it lies
the essence of your testimony.

You see, there's a purpose stitched into every:
problem, a ministry born from every mishap, and a.
calling carved out of every crisis. When the
Apostle Paul penned those words to the Romans, he,
was familiar with tribulation. He knew the sting,
of the shipwreck, the isolation of imprisonment,
and the pain of persecution. Yet, he held fast to
the conviction that everything he faced was
reorienting him to the will of the Master.

Beloved, I charge you to stand in this knowing) stand with the assurance that God is meticulously weaving your life into a tapestry of His design. Every thread, every color, every knot is a part of a larger picture, one that you may only fully understand when you step into eternity and see it from Heaven's vantage point. But until that day, trust in the Artist. Trust in his strokes. Trust in His vision for your life.

You might be facing financial ruin, a health diagnosis that bears no good news, or perhaps your relationships are frayed at the edges. It may seem the devil has you cornered with no way out. But right there, in what appears to be your Gethsemane moment, remember Jesus. Our Savior was not spared the cup of suffering, but through His agony emerged our salvation. Through His unfair trial, we found righteous judgment. Through His death, we claimed eternal life.

The trials you face today could be the very events that lead you to fulfill your God-given destiny tomorrow. Joseph's pit experience led to the palace. Daniel's moment in the lion's den

showcased God's power to shut the mouths of lions.
The silence in the face of your lions could be
the prelude to your loudest victory yet what seems
like defeat could be the setup for your break.
Have faith that your Creator is not oblivious
to your pain or ignorant of your distress; in
fact, His omnipotence never sways. Beneath the
chaos, there is a divine order, beneath the pain,
there is a hidden promise, beneath the defeat,
there is pending victory.

In this very moment, claim Romans 8:28 over
your life. Stand upon the rock of this truth,
knowing and declaring that all things, not some,
but all are working for your good. Wrap yourself
in this truth, let it be the shield that quenches all
the fiery darts of the enemy. And remember,
the good that God is working toward is not limited
by our narrow perspective of what good looks like
It is the ultimate good, the eternal good, the
good designed to bring you into alignment with
His purpose.

As a child of the King, you have been called
according to His purpose - not to a life devoid
of pain, but to one that uses pain to shape you
more like Christ. So when it feels like the enemy'
is winning, stand still and see the salvation of ,

the Lord. Your current situation may not resemble good, but God is the master of transformation, wielding the power to repurpose the enemy's plan. In other words, turn everything around that the enemy thought he was going to do to you, into His divine plan over your life.

My fellow believers, this is a divine invitation for you to lean not on your own understanding but to experience our Heavenly Father's almighty reassurance. For in doing so, we grasp that although Satan may aim for our downfall, the Lord plan is for our uprising. Rise, then, with faith. Rise with the confidence that you do not fight alone, that your battles are portals to blessings, that your tests are the precursors of a testimony.

You never know how the Lord will use you because His ways are not our ways. His thoughts, not our thoughts. What I do know, and what scripture affirms to us, is that all things indeed work together for good, and this good crafts us, shapes us, and sends us forth to fulfill our holy' calling. STAND FIRM!

CHAPTER 35 THE TESTIMONY IN THE
DEN OF A COMPLEX TRIAL

Let us imagine ourselves walking the path of righteousness, a beacon of hope amidst a world parched for truth. Beloved, while we tread upon this spiritual journey, we must always bear in mind that we may be the living testament read by the eyes of those who have yet to open the Good Book. For in our walk, we embody the Scripture, and through our actions, we impart the gospel.

Consider Daniel, a servant whose allegiance t the Almighty placed him in the vicious jaws of danger. His predicament was a den filled with lions. Back then that was considered as a death sentence if you were thrown into that cage. Despite his circumstances Daniel's heart remained: unwavering in his faith towards God. But what Daniel did not know while he was in the pit was a mighty king who was moved by the integrity and constancy of Daniel's Spirit.
In fact this was the same King forced to throw Daniel into the lions den. King Darius who was also praying for Daniel to make it out of the lions den, Darius was the first to run out to the pit to see if Daniel was still living and there Daniel was •.... not even a scratch found anywhere on his body. The king wept as he witnessed Daniel praise his God uncontrollably.

Darius the king, who had unwittingly cast
Daniel into turmoil, was petitioning the heavens
all night, battling through the veils of the night
hoping for salvation to embrace his servant Daniel
in the morn. As it is written, "Then the king was
exceedingly glad for him, and commanded that they
should take Daniel out of the den." Daniel 6:23
KJV. All along this king was spectating, monitoring
the outcome of Daniels faith.

Herein lies a profound lesson for you to chew
on: eyes are always watching, weighing our
character, testing if we are who we claim to be
in Christ. Our lives might very well be the stage
upon which we are appraised, whether for favor
or scorn, prayer or reprobation.

Now lets address a storm, the one brought about
when a soul named Candy, a creation bearing deep
burdens and a history of struggle, stepped into
the sanctuary. This individual's presence caused
a stir, revealing the weakness where strength was
presumed firm. Many fled the scene, for the spirit
that accompanied Candy was one that few knew how
to confront.

Yet, let us recall the words of Apostle Paul
in Galatians 6:1, that those of us who are
spiritual, should seek to restore one who has
stumbled with a gentle spirit, mindful of our own

susceptibility to fall. In this, there is a
beautiful, albeit challenging, command--to love,
to restore, to lift each other up. And even in
this to keep our hearts set on grace, to replace
judgment with the call to steady those who reel.

Witnessing the ultimate example in our Savior
Jesus Christ, we remember that perfection is His
alone. Our sacred duty lies not in measuring the
wrongs of others but in extending a hand in love.
And if one falls, our response- should not be to
cast further down, but to assist in their rise,
thereby truly embodying the very essence of
Christlike love and compassion.

Therefore, let us draw inspiration from the
unshaken Daniel, who, in the face of impending
demise, stood steadfast. His integrity became
his testimony. May we too carry ourselves in such
a manner that even amidst of our own dens of trial
people are always watching to see how you handle
the situation. For we are living epistles. In each
encounter, may we ask ourselves--what is being
read from the chapters of our lives? Let us live
in such a way that like Daniel, even in the den,
our test becomes our testimony and our mess become
our message. AMEN!

CHAPTER 36 A TIME TO EMBRACE

Beloved, as we stand at the crossroads of time and eternity, there breathes a Spirit through the pages of our lives, speaking in the ebbs and flows of seasons, declaring with divine authority that there is indeed a time for everything under heaven. This truth, birthed from the heart of Ecclesiastes 3, resonates through the ages and arrives at our doorstep today with a message that cannot, that must not, be ignored. Now is the time, more than ever, for a necessary dialogue, a holy conversation that weaves toward the colorful threads of faith and identity. The world as we use to know it has changed.

As we anchor ourselves in the wisdom of Ecclesiastes 3, we recognize that the Preacher speaks of times and seasons. A time to be born, and a time to die; a time to plant, and a time to uproot; a time to weep, and a time to laugh; a time to mourn, and a time to dance. Let it be known that this, my family of faith, is a time for understanding, a time for embracing and a time for healing.

This book is presented to you not as a whisper in the shadows, but as a proclamation in the light. For too long, the doors of dialogue have been closed on matters of gender identity within the church. It is a topic shrouded in misunderstanding, steeped in fear and often marred by prejudice, leaving many of our people to walk

a path of solitude when they ought to be accompanied
by love, fellowship and guidance.
But the Spirit declares that now is the time.
Just as Esther was told that she was brought to
the kingdom for such a time as this, so I tell you
that this conversation is appointed for our age,
for our chapter in the divine narrative. The ones
the church condemn instead of embracing?

Let's dive deep into this chapter of theological
waters with the understanding that our exploration
is grounded in empathy, compassion and truth. For
many within our churches, the reality of traversing
two worlds, 'gender identity and faith' has been
a solitary journey marked by questions that echo
against the silent walls of incomprehension. But
dear saints, God is in the business of tearing down
walls and building bridges.

As followers of Christ, we are called to embody
the love that Jesus himself showed at every turn.
who paused at the well to speak life into the
Samaritan prostitute, who stopped procession to
honor a woman who touched his garment. Same now, as
then Jesus extends his hands across lines we've
drawn in the sand, to uplift rather than outcast,
to understand rather than ignore.

The time is gone for fear to dictate our action
The book before you seeks to open the wellsprings
of knowledge and pour out wisdom that refreshes
like rain upon a parched land. For the word of
God is living and active, able to enlighten the
eyes of our heart and reveal the breadth of His
majesty that includes all His creation.

We must come to the table with humility,
recognizing our need for the Spirit's guiding.
This is a Kairos moment, a divine appointment
where we must seize the opportunity for growth,
reconciliation and unity. As children mimicking
the very heart of the Father, it is our duty to
journey alongside every soul, to lift up rather
than condemn, to extend grace as freely as we have
received it.

Within these pages you have witnessed the power
of our Lord through stories and testimonies.
Whether you are a theologian, a pastor, a family
member or a friend this book is for you. It is
for those who seek to understand, to love and to
walk in the footsteps of Jesus who left none
behind in His ministry of reconciliation. It is
for those who recognize that truth without love
is void and love without truth is misguided.

So, in the Spirit of Ecclesiastes. let us
discern that there is a season, and now is the
tithe for this book. And to all those who felt
shunned know this you are not excluded from the
promises of God nor the embrace of his people.
Now is the time the season is upon. BE BLESSED!

CHAPTER 37 INVISIBLE SINS

In this walk with the Lord, my beloved brothers and sister friends and family we must recognize that our journeys are not merely shaped by the actions we take but also by the unseen battles waged within the chambers of the heart. As we traverse the unique paths of our existence, as we climb our mountains and cross our rivers, we must be ever - vigilant against the quiet, insidious foes that threaten to disrupt our divine destiny.

Worry, doubt, guilt, jealously, envy all cause you to carry the cross of misunderstanding and often stand in the shadow of society's judgment remember your fight includes combating the invisible sins that find fertile soil within us all.

Understand that doubt is an intruder that seeks to erode the very foundation of our faith about Christ. It comes cloaked in the seductive guise of 'reason' or 'practicality' whispering that our dreams are too vast for our reach, that our identity is a source of error rather than a celebration of divine diversity. But I say to you, let not your heart be shaken by the tremors of doubt. For the Lord our God, He who knew you before you were formed in your mothers womb, calls you by name and says you are His.

How then shall we respond to doubt? By anchoring ourselves in faith, by holding fast to the truth that we serve a God bigger than our questions and merciful enough to guide us through the storms of uncertainty. Remember that it was faith that allowed the blind to see, the lame to walk, and yes, even the dead to rise. Faith sees beyond the limitations of the flesh, and it is by faith we know that each one of us is a unique expression of God's handiwork.

Now worry, it is the thief of joy, robbing us of the present while shrouding the future in a mist of bleak foreboding. Worry fragments our attention directing it towards the shadows of 'what ifs' and 'maybes,' rather than the solid ground of 'what is'--the promises of God. Worry is a sin because it signifies a lack of trust in God's provision and plan. But family, as you confront the societal pressures and personal questions, I urge you to cast your cares upon the Lord, for His yoke is easy and His burden is light. Do not worry for tomorrow, for tomorrow will worry for itself. Each day has enough trouble of its own.

Jealousy, that green-eyed monster, often rears its head when we compare our journeys to those of others. It whispers lies of inadequacy, suggesting that God's blessings are somehow unfairly

distributed. But know this God has crafted your
path with the precision of a master artisan. When
jealousy attempts derail your path with comparisons
look instead to the blessings in your own hands,
the ones God has specifically chosen for you. In
His kingdom, there is no room for jealousy, for we
all serve a role in His grand design.

And envy, its malicious cousin, it incites us
to covet what is not ours and blinds us to our
divine inheritance. Envy diminishes our capacity
to love, for we cannot genuinely rejoice with our
people when our hearts simmer with desire for
their portion. Envy is particularly profound in the
context of daily experiences, where societal
privileges may seem unevenly allocated. But take
heart, for our God is a God of justice and equity,
and each of us is given what we need according to
His perfect wisdom. Let us cultivate a heart of
contentment and a spirit that celebrates the
victories of others as if they were our own.

Remember, the enemy wishes for you to live in
constant battle with these invisible sins, but the
word teaches us to walk by the Spirit, and you
will not gratify the pitfalls of the flesh. Therefore,
with the armor of God firmly in place, with
the helmet of salvation and the shield of faith,
stand against these invisible adversaries and
runway walk in the joy of Christ being your Savior.

Let us then uproot these sins of doubt, worry, jealousy and envy. Planting instead the seeds of faith, peace, love and contentment. Let the fruit of the Spirit define our lives, not the weeds of the adversary. Let us live unbound by the yoke of this world, for Christ has set us free, and we shall not be burdened again by a yoke of slavery to sin, visible or invisible.

Now shift gears with me as we focus on this wakeup call through scripture guided by a compass pointing not to north, but toward the eternal warmth of grace and truth. For you *see*, the narrative of sin is not told to anchor us in guilt but to liberate us from the shackles that hinder our ascension towards a life abundant in virtue.

Imagine if you will, a student of conviction sitting in a bible study, brimming with fervor, when one preacher with a zeal characteristic of a prophet of old, he declares unto each soul, pointing us out one by one asking "Do you know what your sin is?" A statement not of judgment, but a mirror held before the face, reflecting as if we must confront our sin right then and there. So Brother Gerald quickly inserted "Do you know what your fruit is? Then hinted "it begins with L for love."

Herein lies the wisdom of the ages for the reason Jesus came to sum the law up in one word. The understated truth that while preachers may speak of sin, it is but the starting point of our journey. Sin is the tempest that tests our ships at sea; awareness of it prompts us to seek refuge in the harbors of God's mercy. Preachers illuminate the paths we've tread astray only so we can recalibrate our compasses to true north--toward love, joy, peace, forbearance, kindness, goodness faithfulness gentleness and self control (book format). These are the fruits of the Spirit and in their cultivation lies our redemption.

Beloved, the accentuation of sin in sermons is not to embitter the soul, but to remind us of the potent cure within our grasp. It is to stir an awakening within, so that we might seek that which bears the sweetest of nectar--the love that triumph over all transgressions. It is in the very act of repentance and the acknowledgment of our need for salvation that a grand transformation occurs. The preacher's call is rot one of condemnation but of conviction urging us toward the sanctification process that molds us into the very likeness of Christ.

As we navigate our way through this world, let us remember that the focus of our spiritual leaders is to guide us toward the true essence of our faith--the love that arose on the third day.

the love that cast out all fear, the love that
sees beyond the blemishes of mankind to the heart
yearning for sanctity.

So let us rise, not with hearts laden with the
weight of sin but with spirits buoyed by the
recognition of our growth in love. For in love,
we find the greatest commandment and the purest
expression of the divine. This love, which began
on the cross, continues within us--the ultimate
fruit from which all others emerge, nourishing
us and guiding us to walk in the footsteps of
our Savior.

Let us embrace this compass of conscience,
steering away from the siren call of sin and
toward the fruitful orchard of the Spirit. For
it is by this navigation we become not just hearer
of the word but doers who cultivate the orchard of
God's love in our hearts and in the world around
us. In this understanding, the role of sin in our
teachings become clear--it is a reminder a point
of reference, a catalyst for change. And once
acknowledged, it pales in comparison to the beauty
and the power of the fruit we bear when we walk
in love, rooted in the soil of God's magnificent
Grace. AMEN? YES, AMEN AND GOD BLESS.

CHAPTER 38 THE ETERNAL FLAME

Look around you, my dearly beloved. The world we navigate so meticulously in a constant state of flux, yet the mandates of heaven remain unchanging. Prayer is not an optional accessory that we can afford to overlook; it is one of the most potent tools, a cornerstone in the life of every believer. For therein lies one of our premier defense mechanisms against the wiles of the enemy--in prayer, we find ourselves shielded in spiritual warfare.

The Scriptures implore us to "pray without ceasing," and herein lies a profound mystery, and a heavenly strategy. Within the Old Testament, a fire offering was kindled, never to be extinguish ed; it burned continually upon the altar in a perpetual act of worship. In these contemporary times, the eternal flame is within us its the Holy Spirit, ablaze with unceasing intercession. The Holy Spirit prays even in moment when our conscious minds are at rest. Oh, what a glorious truth it is that the Spirit Himself makes makes intercession for us with groanings which cannot be stopped!

As we lift up our hearts and petitions to our Lord Jesus Christ we do so with a decree of faith proclaiming the answer already secured by the finished work of the cross. Whether united corporately in prayer or engaged in personal communion with God, recognize this: the war we are engaged in is not against flesh and blood. Once you have made peace with Christ, affirming your faith in His unwavering promise to fight your battles. Be steadfast in this knowledge; in times of need, do not waver--call upon the name of the Lord.

Let me tell you, it matters not where you are or the hour upon your clock when the need to pray washes over you. You may find yourself in places of confusion, places where you very identity might be challenged. But let this be a clarion call to your heart--that true worship, true connection with our Creator is bound to neither time nor space.

Understand, precious ones, that our journey with Christ is not about adhering to a set of religious doctrines, but about fostering a personal, intimate relationship with Him. It's about setting aside time to commune with Christ, with a pure heart as your focal point. Throughout your Christian journey, recall that it is essential to exercise the discernment of your surroundings, always keeping the gaze of your heart fixed upon Jesus and His sacrifice. Consider this: when engaging in corporate prayer--as was the case with a believer who sought intercessory prayer from a former love it is critical that the atmosphere remain one of understanding and compassion. When discord arises and some depart from fellowship, take it as a lesson on the journey. The essential truth we must cling to is the Gospel of Jesus Christ and His crucifixion. Let not other narratives diminish the clarity of this truth, for in the kingdom of heaven the worries of this world shall fade away, leaving, only the most pertinent question: Have you accepted Jesus Christ?

Be cautious, my beloved church, for the adversary is crafty, cunning in ways that can lead the focus away from Christ and onto His followers. This is a vile tactic--one we must be vigilant against as we progress into the future. Do not be deceived or carried astray by the shifting sands of doctrine that seek to dismantle the unity and focus of the Church.

In closing this chapter, remember this dear one: Your journey in faith is unique, a personal narrative woven by the hands of the Divine. Embrace your identity, your calling, living as a testimony to the transformative love of Jesus Christ. Being a Christian, or anyone for this matter is not a disqualification from the love and power of prayer. God looks upon the heart, and it is through an unceasing, fervent communion with Him that our true identity in Christ will be revealed and affirmed.

So let us with one accord and full assurance, pray without ceasing. Let us fan into the flames the gift of the Holy Spirit within, for as we march forward, it is unity and in prayer that we will overcome the trials and celebrate the victories to come. Amen.

Family never forget the fire that burns within you. May God Continue to Bless You! Amen!

CHAPTER 39 WORKOUT YOU OWN SALVATION

In the grand design of existence, every stroke of the -Creator's brush, every thread woven into the intricate tapestry of life, is a testament to the inordinate capacity of God's endless grace. I implore you to consider that we are all, undeniably, a 'work in progress', a journey, hemmed with trial and tribulations, joy and despair, often beyond the grasp of our finite understanding. But within the sacred texts of scripture and the tender embrace of divine love, we perceive glimmers of an eternal truth--our deeds, our hearts, our very beings are held in the merciful gaze between us and God.

Beloved seeker, let us delve into this mystery. When you surrendered your life to Christ, a grand exchange took place. Your past, littered with failures and frailty, was absorbed into the abyss of God's forgetfulness. By his stripes, we were healed, and the record of our transgressions, once etched in the stone of judgment, has been washed away, forever forgiven by the blood of the Lamb.

The fabric of faith is dyed with paradoxes as rich and complex as the lives we lead. Scripture urges us to cease from sinning--a call to a higher nature that beckons from within each of us, a reminder that we are fashioned in the holy image of the One who is without blemish. Yet, in this same divine narrative, we find reassurance that

Jesus Christ, in His unbounded mercy, has enveloped our past, present and future missteps in the crimson tapestry of His sacrifice.

As we journey in the present, navigating the ebbing currents of life, we encounter the profound call to "work out our own salvation with fear and trembling" Philippians 2:12. Oh what divine partnership this is! For it is not a lonesome trek or a quest for perfection through human might but an intimate dance with grace, a step-by-step transformation empowered by the Holy Spirit. As the Spirit enlightens, chastises, and comforts, we are molded, more and more, into the likeness of Christ. Each day presents a new canvas on which God's mercies paint fresh beginnings every day we wake up some did not wake up!

The prospect of our future, veiled in the mists of time, may seem daunting, yet it holds an 1 immutable promise: when Christ returns, we shall 1 be glorified, caught up in the consummate act of celestial redemption. In this ultimate fulfillment every stain, every scar, is made whole, and our pilgrim identities are transcended; we shall finally and fully reflect the glory of our Maker.

Your struggles, dear one, are not hidden from the all-seeing eye. God is intimately acquainted with the complexities of the human heart. Sin, in its manifold expressions, ranges from the overtly malevolent to the subtly insidious. The gravity of ill-wishing destruction upon another, harboring bitter desires for a neighbor's downfall, or conceiving heinous plots--they are grievously apparent. yet so often, the world is swift to judge and slow to understand, quick to condemn the outward and tardy to discern the inward.

In the discourse of our times, the topic of how do you work out your own salvation has been thrust into the foreground of moral debate. Individuals, those stuck in limbo, in the treacherous waters between societal constructs and inner convictions, endure judgment for mercy existing as their authentic selves. If the Law of Moses has been obviated through the grace of Christ, where then lies the transgression in personal choice? If "there is therefore no condemnation to them which are in Christ Jesus" Romans 8:1, why do we, as believers, impose chain where Christ has pronounced freedom?

The solemn duty before us is not to a person with power to judge the intricate layers of human experience but to extend the hand of fellowship, to draw souls into the embrace of divine love and to trust Christ to work His will in the courts of our heart. If indeed, judgment is without mercy to one who has shown no mercy; yet mercy triumphs over judgment" James 2:13 our efforts must be cloaked in compassion, not constrained by doctrines put forward by authority

As stewards of the gospel, let us fix our gaze upon the mission endowed to us by our Lord--to seek and to save that which was lost. Every person irrespective of appearance, creed or shortcoming is a candidate for the redemptive work of Christ. We are not arbitrators of divine will; rather, we are the vessels of His grace, called to love, to serve and to witness the transformative power of the gospel.

In this walk of faith, let us be reminded that the heart of the matter is a matter of the heart. - Each life is an individual relationship with the Savior, a sacred dialogue that bears no audience. In the quiet recesses where the soul communes with: the Divine, let us not intrude with the heavy footprints of judgment. For some things, indeed, are not for us to work out but for the merciful hands of the Potter, who shapes the clay of our existence into a vessel of honor, fit for His purpose.

There are moments my family when the road becomes weary, the shadows grow long and the presence of the Lord seems but a distant memory. In those times of spiritual drought, you may look around and wonder, "Is truly working in my life? The heavens seem silent, and the warmth of His touch seems to have cooled. But I stand before you to declare with the authority of the Holy Scriptures, that we must, even in the absence of feeling, stand firm in our faith, knowing that God is working behind the scenes.

Consider Joseph, sold into slavery, falsely accused, and tossed into a dungeon. Did God forsake him? No! The Lord was with Joseph, orchestrating his rise to power in the most unexpected ways. Like Joseph, there are children God who face misunderstanding and persecution, so they fall astray often feeling abandoned in the pits of despair. But remember, He who began a good work in you will be faithful to complete it.

You see, it's not about what you feel; it's about what you know in the depth of your soul. The heart is deceptive, fleeting, driven by the winds of emotion. But faith, 'congregation', faith is the rock upon which we stand when the storms rage. It is the assurance of things hoped for, the conviction of things not seen. When you feel the weight of the world upon your shoulders, when society casts doubt upon your walk in Christ remember that the Lord sees you, He knows you, and He loves you with a love that mankind can scarcely comprehend.

We need the church, my beloved. We need each other. There's a sacred energy that flows when God's people gather in His name--a dynamism that cannot be replicated in solitude. We can't isolate the backslider. The Spirit of Individualism whisper lies of self-sufficiency, saying, "You can do this Christian thing on your own." But the truth is we were never meant to walk this path alone.

We can't isolate the backslider. The Apostle Paul tells us in First Corinthians 12 that we are one body with many parts. Each part, each member and each soul is essential to the Body of Christ. Just as the hand cannot say to the foot, "I don't need you," neither can any of us say to the backslider siblings, "we don't need you." For they too bring gifts, insights and a unique perspective that enriches our spiritual family. The enemy desires to isolate us, for in isolation we're vulnerable. But together, we are strong; we are resilient; we reflect the very image of God, in all its diverse splendor.

And so, I call upon the church to open your doors, open your hearts and stand in solidarity with those navigating the _complexities of faith. They are warriors of the spirit, champions of grace seeking to reconcile their inner truth with the divine-truth and they need our support. They need the warmth of our love, the strength of our prayers and the wisdom of our guidance.

Don't be swayed by the ebb and flow and fleeting emotions. Don't be deceived by the quiet whispers that God has abandoned you. And don't be tricked into thinking that the presence of the Most High is only felt in thunder and lightning, for just as Elijah found God not in the wind, not in the earthquake, not in the fire but in the still of a small voice, so too must we be attuned to the subtle workings of the Spirit.

Remember that our Lord Jesus Christ, when praying in Gethsemane, felt the burden of the cup He was to bear. Did He rely on His feelings at that moment? No, He relied on His unwavering trust in the Father. It was in the solitude of prayer that He found strength but it was in the fellowship of His disciples that He found community and support.

In closing, let us come together as one body under Christ and harness the transformative energy of the collective faith. Let us lift up all our voices in prayer and worship, knowing that where two or three are gathered in His name, there He is in the midst of them. To our backsliders know . this: God is working in your life, just as He is in the lives of all His children. Stand Firm in your faith, embrace the fellowship of believers and together let us walk this journey confident that God's love transcends all barriers and binds us eternally as His family. Amen! Amen! and Amen!

CHAPTER 40 WORLDLY WISDOM IS NOT CHRIST WISDOM

Child of God, I want you to ride with me as we delve into the profundity of these words. The term "spoil" does not merely speak to the spoiling of goods, but to the spoiling of the soul, the plundering of your spiritual wealth, and the potential hijacking of our destiny in Christ Jesus To be spoiled as Paul speaks here, is to be led astray, taken captive, carried off as it were from the richness of true doctrine into the barren wasteland of human philosophy and deceit.

Now, let us consider that Paul speaks of philosophy. Philosophy, in and of itself, is not the enemy. It is the pursuit of knowledge, the love of wisdom. But there is a philosophy that comes rooted not in the divine, but in the mere traditions of men. It is a system built on human reasoning and logic that stands apart from the divine revelation of Jesus Christ. It is devoid of the power of the Holy Spirit and while it may be clothed in the garb of intellectualism, it leads to barrenness, for it fails to draw from the living waters of Christ.

Vain deceit - this falsehood, illusion, the magic trick of the enemy trying to divert your eyes from the truth of the Gospel to focus on the fleeting and deceptive practices of this world. Deception can come clothed in many forms, sometimes in the trappings of tradition, or the tradition, or the modernity of new age ideologies that are at odds with the Gospel's truth. Paul admonishes that we stand guarded against such, holding the word of God as our ultimate truth and shield.

He continues, speaking against traditions - not all traditions, but those that are 'of men', those that have not been birthed out of revelation of Christ and the obedience to the Holy Spirit. There are traditions that are structurally unsound, leading one into religious rituals devoid of power. Christ himself spoke against traditions that invalidated the word of God, and so must we have the', discernment to recognize and forsake any tradition" that does not align with the truth of Christ's teachings.

And then there are the "rudiments of the world" The rudiments, the elemental spirits, the basic principles that the world operates on. The rudiments are the ABC's of worldly living, but in Christ, we are called to a higher education, to graduate into the fullness of His grace and truth. But how do we ensure we are not taken captive through these hollow and deceptive philosophies? Child of God, we anchor ourselves in Christ: For in Him "dwelleth all the fullness of the Godhead bodily," as Paul continues in the subsequent verses. Christ is the embodiment of truth, the exact representation of the divine. And we are complete in Him, who is the head over all principality and power.

Therefore, to walk in the truth is to walk in Christ. To walk in the light is to walk in His 1 word. To find our fulfilment is to seek it not in the ideologies of this world, but in •the intimate 1 and profound relationship with Jesus Himself. For every philosophy that does not acknowledge Him as Lord, every tradition that does not glorify his name, and every rudimentary principle that does not lead us closer to His heart is but a shadow compared to the substance that is found in Christ.

Family, we stand amid a cultural crossroad where the very fabric of our faith is being challenged by a secular worldview desperate to categorize the divine wonder of Jesus Christ as ; mere religious experience. But we must not relent we must not surrender our hold on the eternal truth for a passing, philosophically - sound argument.

In this hour, let the wisdom of Colossians 2:8 take root in your heart. Let it stand as a watchman over your soul. Do not be spoiled or taken captive. Rather, be grounded, rooted, and built up in Him. For in Christ, you will find the very essence of life, the very source of wisdom, and the very foundation upon which your faith must stand. Hold fast to Him, beloved, and let no man deceive you with enticing words. For you, Child of God are called to a higher standard, a divine calling, in Jesus Christ our Lord.

As we travel in the complexities of life, we often find our selves bombarded by distractions that can be as annoying as a fly buzzing around in our car while driving. These distractions can come in many forms: fake people who masquerade as friends, the constant barrage of misinformation from the media, google etc.; Even the temptation to prioritize material possessions over spiritual growth plays a part. The saga never ends.

But in this chaotic world, its crucial to remember
that the Holy Spirit is our guide and our protector. Without Him, we would be lost and vulnerable to the whims of the world. The Bible reminds us, "You shall know the truth and the truth shall set you free" John 8:32. In a world where the truth is often distorted, the Holy Spirit is our only reliable source of guidance.

As we go about our daily lives, it's easy to get caught up in the illusion that everything is going well. We may feel like we're on top of the world, but we must be careful not to become complacent. Life is fleeting and before you know it, it can slip away from us. The Bible warns us, "For what will it profit a man if he gains the whole world and loses his own soul?" Mark 8:36

In these times, it's more important that ever to stay focused on our purpose and to prioritize our spiritual well-being. We must not be swayed by the fleeting pleasures of this world, nor must we become distracted by the noise and chaos that surrounds us. Instead, we must stay grounded in our faith and rely on the Holy spirit to guide us through the trials and tribulations that we face.

So, as you go about your day, remember that life is too short to waste on petty distractions or material possessions. Honor the people you love respect those close to you and live for the moment. Don't wait until it's too late; call on Jesus today and let Him guide you through the maze of this world. God Bless!

CHAPTER 41 VENGEANCE IS THE LORD'S

Dear Friends, I want to share with you a powerful truth from Romans 12:19. It says, "Dear beloved, avenge not yourselves, but rather give place unto wrath: for it is written Vengeance is mine, I will repay, saith the Lord. ' Now I know your thinking. Since you've been hurt you've been wronged you want=to take matters into your own hands. You want to get revenge. But let me tell you, that's not your job. That's the Lord's job.

Let me refresh your memory about who this Lord id is Oh, beloved, lend me your ears and let this sink into your spirit mingled with the rugged cross atop Golgotha's hill.

Understand, my brethren, that it was but once-- yes, once--that our Redeemer, the Lamb that was slain, our Jesus, was crucified. That immutable event is etched into the annals of heaven, never to be erased, never to be repeated. It stands as unchangeable as the God who ordained it. The moment He exhaled His last and declared, "It is finished," heaven itself stood still, witnessing the fulfillment of a mission so divine, so pure, that it would ripple across time and eternity.

Imagine with me, if you will, the weight of that proclamation-- "It is finished." The chains of the old covenant began to rattle and collapse as the new dawned--a covenant steeped in grace, showered by mercy, and blood-bought by the Ultimate Sacrifice. With those three words, Jesus sealed the covenant that would break the yoke of sin, crush the sting of death, and fling wide open the gates to eternal life for all who would believe.

As He surrendered to the grave, our Messiah was enacting the grandest of escapes, for in His burial and His magnificent resurrection, death itself was dealt a fatal blow. Oh, the victory that flooded forth from that tomb as the stone rolled away! Death could no longer be the larcenist of our souls, for Christ had emerged the conqueror the beacon of an endless life.

Now, we, made alive in Him, are called--no we are commissioned! to be the very conduits, the ,vessels, the carriers of this gospel of liberation We are to tread the foot-soaked soils of the Old Testament, to honor its prophecies, and revere its types and shadows, but then to lead the lost out of that wilderness into the promised land of New Testament reality. Oh, yes! The Old Testament scriptures, those ancient scrolls, were but the voice crying out in the wilderness, paving the way, preparing the hearts for the Messiah's sojourn to the cross.

There are some among us, beloved, who find themselves still encompassed within the thicket, clinging to the Pentateuch as if it were the sole revelation of God's design. But let U.S not be swayed to remain within the encampment of the initial five, where laws were laid to govern an unruly people, a civilization to be tamed--for it was also where God, in His matchless wisdom, began to weave the prelude to Christ.

The shadow was cast, mighty and unyielding, but through the shadow came the substance, the very essence of salvation through Jesus Christ our Lord. As those shadows showed a figure looms, how much more does the figure itself reveal when it steps into the warmth of the day! And that day has come.

Let's not remain in the twilight, children of God. The brightness of the Son's glory beckons us forward. It is within Him that we live, we move, and have our very being. So let us walk in that life, let us exemplify that freedom, and carry forth that torch which has been entrusted to us. May we alight the path for those still navigating the dim recesses of the former covenant, guiding them to the Messiah--the fulfillment of the law, the embodiment of grace, and the start of our eternal communion with the divine.

That's our Lord we serve a wonderful and magnificent Savior. So, instead of trying to get revenge, we need to trust and believe that the

Lord will take care of it. We need to walk by faith, not by sight. We need to know that no matter who has harmed us, the Lord has our back. He's got our best interests at heart, and He will make sure that justice is served.

Now, I know it's hard to sit back and wait. It' hard to trust that the Lord will take care of the issue. But I want to encourage you to do just that. I Don't try to take matters into your own hands. Don't try to get revenge. Instead, trust the Lord and know that He will handle it.

And let me tell you, when the Lord does handle it, you'll be amazed at how He does it. You'll be amazed at the power and the justice He brings. t And you'll be amazed at how He makes you a believer in His vengeance.

So, dear friends, remember that vengeance is the Lord's. Don't try to take it upon yourself. Trust and believe that He will take care of it. And know that no matter who has harmed you, the Lord has your back Amen?

CHAPTER 42 JESUS SAID "MIND YO BUSINESS"

Let us begin with the tender scene in John 21: 22 particularly with Peter. It is here that Peter in his humanity, diverts from the personal commission Jesus has given him and cast his gaze upon John, questioning what Jesus's intentions was for another disciple. "Lord what about him?" Peter asks, and Jesus, with infinite patience and gentle reproof, restores Peter's focus: "If I will that he remain till I come, what is that to you? You follow me." Clearly Jesus wanted to say "Mind Yo Business".

In a world that often grapples with the complexities of life and the intersectionality of faith and self expression, we must take a moment to consider the teachings of our Lord Jesus Christ and the Apostle Paul. We understand through our scripture that the journey of the next individual soul is multifaceted and nuanced, and within this narrative, the experience of personal choice call for our attention, empathy and understanding.

Come ahead as we unfold the sacred texts and peer into the essence of Christ's love, linking arms with Paul's wisdom to navigate through our own perceptions and embrace the beauty of every Child of God.

As Shepherd of our hearts, Jesus profoundly highlights a key element of our faith journey: the importance of concentrating on our own individual path, our private personal relationship with Christ, rather than becoming distracted or disheartened by the journey of what others are doing. This is a poignant reminder for us as we consider the lives and challenges faced by Christians within our Christian community.

Jesus's response to Peter is an admonishment against comparison and a call to love and embrace the unique story of each believer. Whatever their journey is to us, if not a reflection of the diverse tapestry God weaves with each life? Instead of questioning or judging, we are to love and support, "following" Jesus in His example of unconditional love.

Moving into the epistles of Paul, we wrestle with the application of doctrine and the heartbeat of fellowship among believers. In First Corinthians 4:5, Paul writes, "Therefore judge nothing before the time, until the Lord comes, who will both bring to light the hidden things of darkness and reveal the counsels of the hearts Then each one's praise will come from God." Paul a steward of the mysteries of God, is instructing us to refrain from premature judgment or condemnation.

For it is not within our human purview to discern the complexities of the heart or the depth of ones journey with Christ. Thats His job.

So many Christians, much like the Apostle Paul, are on a challenging road, a road filled with discovery, revelation and sometimes painful misunderstanding. As fellow sojourners seeking to live out our faith authentically, we must heed the call to "judge nothing before time." Our role is to honor each individual's connection to the divine, trusting that the same God who searches hearts and minds is perfectly capable of leading each of His children into the fullness of their purpose and identity in Him.

Consider the transformation of Paul; once Saul, a persecutor of the early church, his experience on the road to Damascus changed him profoundly, awakening him to a greater understanding of God's expansive love and grace. It was personal, it was spiritual, and it bypassed the human inclinations towards judgment and condemnation. Paul's journey, radical and controversial for his time, reminds us that the roads we travel in pursuit of sanctification and truth are often unexpected and uniquely tailored by God.

When we examine the inclusivity of Jesus's message and the expansiveness of Paul's ministry we encounter a synergy in their teachings that calls for love, patience and expectation. The love that does not differentiate, that sees each person as valuable; the patience that allows for growth and learning in the journey of faith; and

the expectation of the transformative work that
God is performing in each of our lives, regardless
of how our paths unfold:

In light of John 21:22 and First Corinthians
4:5 we as brethren as a community of believers
are invited to participate in a narrative that
includes, accepts and validates our family.
They, like us, are engaged in a pilgrimage of
faith--discerning, discovering, and becoming who
they have been called to be. Our response ought
not to be one of judgment or idle curiosity, but
of fellowship, edification and encouragement
each and every time you see your people in Christ.

A renowned preacher, a man of great insight
and profound wisdom, once said, "We need to be
stretched sometimes to the outer limits of our
faith." He understands the journey of growth
requires us to be challenged, to learn from one
another, and to let love, be the driving force
behind our conversations and actions. We must be
willing to be 'stretched' to understand the
entire experience within the context of Christianity,
growing in our faith as we learn to embrace
all members of the body of Christ.

Christianity is not a call to rewrite theology
but to expand our application of it through the

lens of love that Jesus so clearly demonstrated. To live and express loving acceptance doesn't negate the words of Paul or the divinity of Christ; rather, it fulfills the law of Christ, allowing us to "bear one another's burdens, and so fulfill the law of Christ" (Galatians 6:2).

As we step into the light of new understanding let us hold fast to Jesus's admonition and Paul's counsel. Let us look within our own hearts and ask God to guide us in the delicate dance of grace and truth. May we "follow" Jesus into a world where love dictates our actions, where humility is our guide, and where every child of God can find a home in the family of faith.

And so beloved, whenever we are tempted to question another's journey or to cast a stone of judgment, let us remember the beautiful simplicity of Jesus's words: "What is that to you? You follow Me." Let us pursue this divine directive with all our hearts, knowing that in doing so, we honor both the diversity and the unity of the Body of Christ. Let us walk in the footsteps of the Master and in the broad grace of the Apostle Paul, embracing each soul's sacred story, as we journey together toward the horizon of love and acceptance that Christ Himself has set before us.

Now, let's backdoor, The Famous Door, down memory lane in the thriving history of faith, threaded with the stories of men and women whose souls danced gracefully to the rhythm of faith, we find a poignant narrative. It is a chronicle of flawed beings, imperfect and marred by their missteps, yet enveloped by an astonishing grace that defied the very norms of judgment and condemnation. Like a masterful weaver, the Divine touched the strands of their lives, not to untangle every knot of wrongdoing, but to exhibit how those very knots hold the secret of their undeterred faith.

In the dawn of our discourse, let us foregather around the story of David, a man after God's own heart, yet blemished by his own frailty. David was no stranger to fault—his heart soaked of both adoration and transgression. Nevertheless, it was not his moral failure with Bathsheba or the catastrophe that befell his house thereafter that defined his legacy. Rather it was his unwavering faith, his willingness to confront his own brokenness, his psalms of repentance, and his relentless pursuit of righteousness that became the hallmark of his life. David's story echoed through generations, a testament that the faith of a person is not overshadowed by their fall but is made luminous in their rise back to the light of grace.

Just as the Lord did not forsake David, so too did he remember Rahab, the woman marked by her past as a harlot. Yet, it was Rahab's faith, not her history, that scripted her future. By the merit of her belief, she secured a legacy.

that would be-woven with threads of redemption, for she helped safeguard the Israelite spies when they needed refuge. Her lineage stands as witness to the depth of divine acceptance, as she became an ancestor to the very Messiah, whose tapestry of humanity included the vibrancy of her faith, overshadowing the dark threads of her former indiscretions.

My beloved friends, consider the Apostle Peter, a man of impetuous spirit and stout heart, who walked alongside the Savior himself. He declared his loyalty to Christ with vigor, yet he too stumbled, denying Jesus thrice when fear gripped his soul. Yet, the error of his action was not the full measure of the men. Christ, in his boundless love and understanding, restored Peter, commissioning him to shepherd His flock. It was not the denial of Christ that told the tale of Peter's life, but his constant return to the embrace of Christ and the enduing outpouring of his soul to the early church. Peter's faith did not succumb to the shadow of his wrongdoing; rather, it shone more brilliantly, refined through the process of divine forgiveness.

These tales converge in a symphony of sorts, an operatic testament to the soul-stirring truth that our humanity cannot confine the breadth of divine grace. In our modern day pilgrimage, the same vivifying truth applies. The woman battling addiction, the man ensnared in deceit--each child of God is not defined by their flaws but by their unyielding grip on belief.. Their faith,

imperfect though it may be, becomes the defining
narrative of their life journey.

In our communities, in our churches, under
the steeples that point to the heavens as if
directing our gaze upward, we find souls laden
with blunders yet pressing forward in faith.
Their wrongdoings are but chapters in their
stories, not the ending. It is paramount to
understand that in the grand scheme of redemption
our transgressions are but platforms for grace to
exhibit its power. The adulterer, the liar, the
envious heart--each one can experience transformation,
not by the mere absolution of their acts,
but by the relentless pursuit of a life tethered
to faith.

My brethren, do we not see it? It is in the
soil of imperfection that the seeds of faith
germinate robustly, watered by tears of repentance
and cultivated by the hands of a Creator who sees
beyond our failures. The Father's judgment is not
a ledger of misdeeds but a cherished list of
moments when, despite our erring ways, we have
chosen to believe, to trust, and to hold fast
to the hope we profess.

So let us pen our individual chapters in the
knowledge that while we may stumble, our faith
in redemption defines us. Our redemption song
does not start with an account of how we have faith

but rather with a melody of how, through our faith, we embraced the grace offered to us so freely. God does not discard us for our iniquities Instead, He crafts masterpieces from the rubble of our brokenness, as long as we remain steadfast in our devotion.

In the closing of this chapter in our spiritual sojourn, may we take solace in the company of fellow believers, past and present, who journey similarly upon this path. Although we are not perfect vessels, we hold a treasure within-- faith that outshines our frailties. Let not a single wrinkle upon your spirit be cause for despair, for in the kingdom of our Lord, each blemish is but a space for His grace to fill and for His glory to shine ever brighter.

Hold onto your faith, dear saints, for it is the very essence that carries you beyond judgment and into the boundless embrace of everlasting grace. May Peace be with you! God Bless!

CHAPTER 43 EVERYDAY IS HOLY

Beloved, we have come together, gathered in His name, to delve into the sanctity of celebration and the revelations of our holy days. Across denominations, among the various threads of the tapestry that is Christianity, we honor certain days as high and holy. We speak of Easter, Christmas, Pentecost, and Good Friday with due reverence Yet, as we walk this journey of faith, it is imperative to understand that God is not constrained by our calendars, nor is He bound by the sequence of days we deem special. For in the eyes of the Lord, every day is a vessel for the sacred, and every moment is ripe for His glory.

Let me tell you, beloved, that your breakthrough need not wait for Easter, nor must your moment of redemption arrive only on Christmas. The presence of the Lord dwells with us perpetually, coursing through our everyday lives like the eternal rivers of living water. When we awaken to the truth that every day we draw breath is a day designated by God, we unlock a cascading celebration that is not limited to the marked dates on our calendars.

You see, time is God's creation, and He presides above it. Holidays and holy days serve as markers, temporal lighthouses guiding us through the seasons of faith. They are beautiful; they are necessary. They remind us of the pivotal event that define the essence of our belief--the birth death, and resurrection of Jesus Christ, our

cornerstone, our hope. But they are not the
alpha and omega of our worship. Our praise should
not be relegated to these appointments alone.

It was on an ordinary day, not prescribed by
the rituals of mankind, that the Lord spoke to
Moses from a burning bush. On an average day, a
day like any other, the widow of Zarephath
encountered a miraculous provision. And on a day
unsuspected, a nondescript day in the grand
scheme of history, a virgin named Mary received
an angel's visit, setting in motion our redemption
story.

In the hustle and bustle of life, we often
seek markers, milestones-- a sign that we are
moving forward. Still, in the anticipation of
these celebratory days, do we not neglect the
opportunities presented in the still, small
moments of the mundane? For in these moments,
God is at work, molding our character, shaping
our faith. He is as much in the Tuesday morning
sunrise as He is in the Sunday morning sermon.

Consider the Lord's Supper, my friends. As we
break bread and sip from the cup in remembrance
of Him, are we to consign this profound act of
communion to a particular day? No! Our Savior
said, "Do this in remembrance of Me." He did not
say, "Do this on the Sabbath of each quarter."

Any day is ripe for this holy communion, any moment fit for reflection on His sacrifice.

Let us break the shackles of the ordinary. Let us awaken to the sacredness enveloping us always. The same power that rolled the stone away from the tomb abides in the Monday markets and the Thursday theaters. That power is not awaiting an invitation engraved on holiday cards it is ever-present, knocking at the doors of our Monday to Friday, beckoning us to recognize that within these days lies the potential for divine encounter.

By shedding the limitations we impose upon our celebrations, we step into a life of continuous worship. Our joy is not postponed until December, nor does our gratitude lie dormant until November. Today, irrespective of its place on the timeline of human custom, we can lift our hands in thanksgiving for His eternal love.

As Psalm 118:24 declares, 'This is the day the Lord has made; let us rejoice and be glad in it." Each day, bestowed upon us with the grace and artistry of our Maker, is a masterpiece awaiting our recognition. The Monday blues the Wednesday lull, the Friday frenzy--all are infused with the potential for jubilation and reverence....

So, I call upon you, precious child of God, Don't wait for the next holiday to express your adoration. don't hold back your praise until the calendar dictates its time. Embrace the liberating truth that our God is not confined by dates or seasons. His triumph requires no commemorative event to validate its pertinence.

Together, let us reshape our understanding of what is holy and what warrants celebration. For when we inhabit a state of perpetual praise, every day becomes a holy day, every moment an opportunity for exaltation, and every breath a testament to the God who transcends time.

Remember, dear ones, the sacred can be found in every sunrise, every smile, every act of kindness, regardless of the hour. Our lives, our worship, our unceasing celebration--they are not to be boxed into occasions. They are free; they are boundless; they are eternal, just like the Father's love for us.

So, rise up, believers! Let the joy of the Lord erupt in your heart today, tomorrow, and every subsequent day the Lord grants us. Sing, dance, and live out the gospel with fervor, not just on the holidays, but on all days. For in doing so, we honor the God of eternity, whose glory outshines every festive day on earth. Amen my friend! I feel the need to bring to your attention the meaning of Amen!

It is this very essence of thankfulness that you turn your attention to a word, just one, a powerful affirmation, that resonates through the corridors of our worship and infuses our collective consciousness with spiritual assent. That word, my friends, is "Amen." A word we so often use.

Do you know when you utter "Amen", it is not just a habitual conclusion to our prayers; it is the seal, the confirmation, the culmination of ,our faith, promulgated into the atmosphere, boldly declaring our alignment with the divine utterance that has been spoken. Amen stands as a sentinel at the gates of our belief, affirming that we have heard the word of God and we stand ready to march into action harmoniously with its decree.

But let us delve deeper into the profound layers of "Amen." This is not just a perfunctory echo or a passive nod of acquiescence. No, when you say "amen", you are invoking the very power of agreement that holds the universe in its grand design. You are aligning your spirit with the purpose and intent of the Almighty. When you say "Amen", you are entering into a covenant, a divine pact that states you are in accord, hand in hand, lifting each other up in the faith that has been professed.

Saying "Amen" is akin to laying down the bricks of faith with the mortar of conviction. Each time we say it, we build upon our spiritual edifice, creating a fortress of belief that can withstand the storms of doubt and the winds of uncertainty. "Amen" is not merely a word; it is the sword and shield of our devotion, a testament that we will undeniably rise above any trials and tribulations that may come our way.

"Amen" resonates with the frequency of truth. It transcends barriers, unites us across differences, and serves as a shared language of hope and perseverance. It is a declaration that while we may at times walk through valleys of shadow, we do not fear. We are resolute because "Amen" is an affirmation of unseen victories already won on our behalf.

And oh, my brethren, when you say "Amen", let it not be a mere whisper but a roar--a thunderous affirmation that reverberates through the halls of eternity. Let it be a battle cry, announcing to the principalities and powers that be that we have not only heard the promise but that we are steadfast in its proclamation. We stand ready to see it manifest in the fullness of God's timing and richness.

Let us also understand that the gravity of "Amen" reaches both the heights of jubilation and the depths of solemn vow. When the preacher articulates the profound depths of gospel truth, when a prayer is lifted up for healing, deliverance, or grace, when a testimony is given that stirs the deepest wellsprings of the soul, your "Amen" is a vessel of worship that carries those declarations into the manifestation realm. It is our spiritual endorsement that turns the unseen into a visible outpouring of His blessings.

In conjunction, "Amen" is our shared responsibility. For when we speak it, we take ownership of what follows. We acknowledge that with God's promises are "Yes" and "Amen". Therefore, when we pronounce "Amen", we participate in a divine exchange, one where heaven touches earth and the extraordinary infiltrates the ordinary.

In this vast tapestry of existence, with all its complexities, "Amen" stands triumphant as simplicity itself. It does not require eloquence or grandeur; it yearns for sincerity and belief. When someone in need reaches out for prayer, and they say "Amen" realize that you are evoking the compassionate heart of God, aligning your spirit with the one who lifts the downtrodden and sets captives free. With every "Amen", we are reinforcing our solidarity with the hurting, the broken, and the seeker.

So let every "Amen" that departs your lips be a bold affirmation, a sanctified agreement, and a proclamation of your unwavering faith in the Almighty. Allow your "Amen" to be as the ringing bell of truth, signaling to all that when the sord of God is spoken, His children stand in unified accord, ready to witness His power, grace and love unfold in magnificent and miraculous ways.

Therefore, my people, as we go forth this day and every other day henceforth, let us say "Amen" with conviction, let us say "Amen" with expectation and let us say "Amen" with the fullness of our hearts, for in that powerful syllable, we acknowledge the certainty of God's faithfulness. And as we continue in our journey, may our "Amen" be more than a word--it must be our banner, our seal and our song. May our "Amen" be the sound of agreement that lights the world, that showcases the glory of God in us, and through us, for all to see and believe. Amen and Amen and Amen!

CHAPTER 44 THE ESSENCE OF FAITH AND FRUIT

Jesus, the High Priest, the Wonderful Counselor the Anointed One, the Lamb, a formidable orator and spiritual leader, often spake of the imagery of sowing and harvesting to illustrate the integral principles of the followers life. As we embrace the complexities of modern spirituality, particularly the intersection where true Christianity meets fake Christianity, Jesus teachings on faith becomes the residential relevance for this wicked and stiff necked generation.

In the domain of 2024 hereinafter Christianity, faith takes on a twofold dimension. Firstly, it is the belief in a loving, inclusive God who sees beyond the flesh and embrace all creations. Secondly, it is the personal conviction that all in their unique identity bare a sacred truth that is often tested by societal norms and religious etiquette.

See, my dear, the seed of faith is planted when an individual comes to the realization of their true self. It is a quiet knowing, a divine whisper that validates your belief. But for this seed to grow, it requires an environment fertile with compassion.

Jesus often spoke parables about the obstacles

that believers would face - doubts that attempt
to wither the seedlings of faith. We as Christian
are no strangers to such tribulations. However,
doubts can come in the form of discrimination,
prejudice and misinterpretation of scripture
that seek to invalidate an individuals faith
within the community.

Watering the belief requires continual
reinforcement of one's spirituality and personal
truths. The act of worship, prayer, and scriptura
contemplation are all vital practices in solidifying
the foundation of belief against the erosive forces of
doubt. This is the rain that sustains growth, ensuring
that the tender roots of faith dig deep into the soil
of conviction.

Jesus is a proponent of the strength found
in communal ties. For everyday Christians,
community means a congregation, a family of
believers who recognize and affirm each other's
belief. The Body of Christ require the soil of
an acceptable community for everyone to thrive
in their spirituality. This soil is enriched by
the mutual sharing of experiences, the collective
worship, and the joint pursuit of understanding
God's love. Jesus vision of a thriving faith
community is one in which diverse members
support one another, share in the joys and
struggles of growth, and bear fruit that enrich
not only their lives but also the world around

them. The light enables faith to flourish is the understanding and interpretation of scripture. Jesus often emphasizes the need for illuminated scripture, where the Word is not just read but also comprehended in its context. For Christians this light shines differently; it must disperse the shadows cast by misinterpreted texts used to marginalize and condemn.

An enlightened reading of scripture see beyond verses taken out of context to justify exclusion. Instead, it seeks passages that affirm God's love for all, such as the message of Galatians 3:28 - "there is neither Jew or Greek, there is neither slave nor free, there is no male or female, for you are all one in Christ Jesus." In this divine light, all Christians can grow, understanding that their identity does not separate them from God's love or the fellowship of believers.

Pruning is also a necessary part of spiritual growth. It involves facing challenges and allowing them to shape and strengthen one's faith rather than to destroy it. All believers encounter specific hardships, such as societal stigma, personal reconciliations of faith and identity. Note: When I speak of identity its not always related to sexual preference. Identity is also how people want to conform to the latest technology, trend or phenomenon just to fit in instead of being your true self in Christ. Some even search for belonging within religious sphere that has historically rejected them.

The pruning process involves tough questions and periods of spiritual dryness, yet it is often through this pruning that Christians find their most profound convictions and emerge with a tenacious grip on their beliefs. Their trials become testimonies of resilience, an integral part of their spiritual narrative that speaks to the steadfastness of faith.

The ultimate expression of faith is the fruit it bears--how belief manifests in the life of a believer. For the average Christian, the fruit of faith is living authentically in accordance with their true selves and using their experiences to encourage and uplift others. Being fruitfulness is not just personal success, but the ability to impact the lives of others positively.

The fruit of Christian spirituality can be immensely transformative. They are seen in acts of courage, in the pursuit of justice, and the offering of hope to other marginalized individuals. This fruit then becomes sustenance for those still struggling. Their visible lives bearing fruit . will provide evidence that God's love is still at work transcending human-imposed boundaries.

In this exploration of faith and fruit in the tone of Christianity we recognize parallels to the spiritual teachings of Jesus. Through acceptance, belief, communal support, enlightened scripture and the transformative power of

CHALLENGES, Christians are called to sow the seeds
of faith, nurture the soils of their spiritual life
and harvest the fruits of their walk with God,
contributing to the vibrant tapestry of Christian
faith.

Family I cannot expound enough on a Harvest of
the Spirit. This was and still is Jesus focal
point not sin. Sin is just another way of inserting
the Law of Moses into your conscious. In the
depths of our souls, there is another calling, a
yearning, a divine mandate bestowed upon each of
us, to bear fruit - fruit that is good, enduring
and reflective of the Most High's boundless love.
Hear me when I say that God does not operate on
the timelines and restrictions of seasons that
man knows, for He expects us to bear this sacred
fruit in season and out. Our character must
blossom with the fruit of the Spirit, and the
most luscious fruit among these, the key that unlocks
the very essence of God's character within us, is
love.

Dear Reader, love is not merely a sentiment; it
is the bedrock upon which all virtues are built.
It is the sun to which the fruits on the tree of
our lives turn their faces. And atop these branches
joy that radiant main fruit - is perpetually
withing the grasp of the enemy. Satan prowls,
seeking to snatch it away, for he knows joy is the
connective tissue between the happiness we seek
and the blessings we receive. We must stand guard
of our joy zealously, for it is precious and

wholesomely divine.

Let us then speak of peace - the fruit that provides solace and sanctuary when tempests rage about us. In the midst of our trials and tribulations, it is the serene assurance that whispers steadily into our hearts, "fear not, for Christ is always with you." Peace is the anchor in the storm, the eye amidst the hurricane of life, reminding us that in His presence, there is refuge.

And what of long-suffering? This fruit often: tastes bitter to the tongue, but oh, how sweet is its nourishment to the soul! Long-suffering gives us the fortitude to extend the hand of forgiveness to those who have wronged us, recognizing that our transgressions too have been pardoned in multitude through the ceaseless grace of Christ. For forgiveness is a path that must be trodden in both directions - we cannot seek it without also being willing to give it.

Consider goodness - it challenges us to display virtue in the face of pettiness, to rise above the lowliness of ignorable acts, and to remain steadfast in our commitment to what is right. Goodness is not naive; it is wisdom dressed in simplicity, choosing to wear grace rather than grievances.

Then there is faith - the very essence of our conviction; the substance of things hoped for, the evidence of things unseen. Faith does not judge, for it understands that each journey is unique and each struggle is a deeply personal battle waged within the chambers of the human heart.

What shall we say of temperance, that venerable fruit which equips us with restraint in the presence of excess and indulgence? It is the strength 4 to abstain, to hold our peace when witnessing the spiritual infancy of our carnal brothers and sisters so that we may yet encourage, lift and bear witness to the Light.

Age, my friends, is but a mere number - a figure that no more defines wisdom than the clock defines time itself. The. gentle are young at hears for they possess the quality of being as tender as lambs, unblemished by the world's chaos, untouched by the abrasiveness of strife.

Meekness walks hand in hand with gentleness, bestowing upon its bearer the grace to be humble to recognize our own vulnerabilities, and to treat others with a compassion that transcends human understanding, especially when faced with the invisible battles of mental health.
All of these fruits - love, joy, peace, long suffering, gentleness, goodness, faith, meekness and temperance - they flow through love, which

without question, the primary fruit. It is this love that delineates our authenticity as followers of Jesus Christ. For now, it is not the outer appearance that govern our actions, but it is the inner man, the renewed, regenerated spirit that controls the newborn within us. Let us walk in the Spirit, and thus, not fulfill the lust of the flesh. let us be abundant, let us overflow, and let us always bear the fruits that testify to the wondrous transformation bestowed upon us by our Savior.

Remember, children of the Most High God, the fruits of the Spirit are not seasonal - they are perennial, everlasting and potent. Let us tend to our spiritual orchards with care, nurturing these divine gifts, so that we may offer a boundless harvest of righteousness and love to the world who desperately needs it. God Bless You All!

CHAPTER 45 THERE IS NO REPRODUCTION IN HEAVEN

My beloved, in the realm of the everlasting, in the celestial corners of heaven, there is an order that surpasses our understanding--one where the biological impulses and social constructs that we wrestle with do not apply. In heaven, there is no reproduction. This is a notion that may unsettle the frameworks by which we live, but it is a profound truth that liberates us from the transient and escorts us into the eternal.

Now, why does this matter? It matters because in the eyes of our Creator, our spirits are the currency of eternity. It is not the flesh that ascends; it is the spirit that soars. The deeds done in the body, the love shared, the compassion extended--these are the emblems of our spirits. When we stand before the throne, it is not our flesh or our earthly roles that are adjudicated; it is the essence of our spirits--whether good or bad, noble or wanting.

Consider how we navigate this world. We are birthed into categories and labels that prescribe our paths: male and female, rich and poor, young and old. So often, these divisions dictate our worth, our potential, and our contribution. But let me remind you, in the divine tapestry of the Almighty, these distinctions are ephemeral. Our

Lord is not a respecter of persons in the way we might fear. God searches the heart, He measures the spirit.

For in Heaven, you will be recognized for the love you gave, for the forgiveness you extended, for the burdens you bore in His mighty name. These deeds that echo in eternity--these are the signature of a good spirit. And conversely, a spirit that has harbored bitterness, that has sown division, that has turned from the light of truth, is one that carries the weight of those choices beyond the veil.

Now, I hear you. On this terrestrial plane, we grapple with the flesh, with knowing our true selves and finding our place in the symphony of life. Some find solace in their expression; others find it a source of profound struggle. But take heart, for in the final chapter, when the mortal coil is unwound, our flesh are gone as we transcend. God's love embraces every nuance of who we are.

And let us not be deceived: there will be good and bad in all walks of life--that much is certain. From the highest palace to the humblest street, you will find generosity and cruelty, compassion and indifference. But do not let the actions of others disturb your spirit. Instead, let it be a call to rise above, to exemplify the grace that has been afforded to you.

Look around, my brothers and sisters--our world is blooming with diversity, with hearts beating in various shades of conviction and truth. Yet, hear me when I say: in the realm of eternity, it is not our societal labels that define us; it is our spirits' alignment with the divine will. Our readiness to walk in love, to seek justice, to uphold mercy: these are the measures of our souls.

Therefore, let us strive to nurture spirits that are good: buoyant with faith, brimming with hope, overflowing with charity. For when we shed this mortal skin, when we step across Jordan into that land of endless day, it is our spiritual legacies that will speak for us--not the echoes of the flesh, not the whispers of physical reproduction, but the loud proclamation of our love-infused actions.

Embrace this understanding as we continue to walk the path laid before us. Remember that whether in moments of solitude or in the hustle and bustle of life, your spirit is cultivating its legacy--one thought, one action, one heartbeat at a time. What will your spirit echo in eternity?

So let us look forward to that day--not with trepidation, but with the assurance of those who have lived and loved in the light of divine truth. Let us live as those who know that in heaven, our spirits will resound with the life we've lived, the love we've shared, and the faith we've held fast.

In this knowledge, let your hearts be at peace. With the complexities and the beauty it holds in this life and pale in comparison to the profound purpose we possess as children of God--spirit beings designed to resonate with His eternal love. And on that day, we shall fully understand, as we are fully known, and we will dwell in the house of the Lord forever, beyond bounds of earth-bound definitions, in perfect unity and harmony with our Creator.

You must know that when God spoke the world into existence, He did so with love and intentionality creating humanity in His divine image. In every face, every story, every unique expression of self, God's signature is unmistakably present.

Beloved, remember that you were once dead in your transgressions and sins. We all were. It is not our spirit or fleshly expressions that once deadened us; it was our human nature, severed from the Living Vine. The world tells us many stories about who we should be, whispering lies of our value predicated on our alignment with its transient norms and expectations. Societal norms change, but the word of the Lord endures forever.

Pause and see how Paul illuminates our condition without Christ, we are without hope and without God. But the story doesn't end there. The heart of the gospel echoes into the vastness of human diversity and declares in thunderous tones: "But God...." Grace interrupts our narrative, flipping the script from alienation to adoption, oppression to liberation, condemnation to celebration. "But God, who is rich in mercy, because of His great love with which He loved us...made us alive together with Christ."

Listen believers, the narrative of Ephesians Chapter 2 is your narrative. It speaks of resurrection power, breathing life into the very core of who you are in God's eyes. Your identity in Christ is not a secondary, peripheral matter--it is primary, it is central, it is grounding. In a world that questions your worth, in systems that challenge your dignity, hear the truth of the gospel affirming your place at the table of fellowship. You are God's workmanship; fearfully and wonderfully remade in Christ Jesus to accomplish good works, which were prepared in advance for you, for such a time as this.

How dare the accuser point a finger at you when the hands that molded you are marked with the scars of sacrificial love! The old order of sin and shame has been deposed; in Christ, we are part of the new creation. "For through Him we both have access by one Spirit to the Father." Through Him--there is no other way. One Spirit, uniting us all in the embrace of the Father, who does not cast anyone away because of our diverse ways of manifesting His image.

Together, as one body in Christ; the walls of division crumble; Jew and Gentile, slave and free, He came and preached peace to you who were far away and peace to those who were near.

In Him, we are being built together into a dwelling place for God. Think about that for a moment. In all our glorious diversity, in the magnificent tapestry of humanity woven by the hand of God, the Spirit delights to dwell. Every heartbeat, every breath, every soul is a testament to the Creator's joy in His creation. 0 Child of God, do not let anyone diminish the beauty of your existence or the legitimacy of your journey. You are integral to the dwelling place God is building--a temple sacred and diverse, resplendent with the colors of His infinite spectrum.

When feelings of inadequacy or the bitter sting of rejection assails you, anchor yourself in the riches of His mercy. You were saved by through faith--not because of how well you fit into the expectations of others, but because of the unmerited favor poured out unto you in loving abundance. You are His masterpiece, engraved with the brushstrokes of divine purpose. Wear your identity in Christ with nobility and courage, for it is the truest thing about you.

My beloved, let us then walk into the light of this revelation, arms open wide to embrace every child of God, as part of the redeemed community. Let us tear down the high places of ignorance and build bridges of understanding. For our fight is not against flesh and blood, but against principalities and powers that seek to deny the image of God in any of His children.

In conclusion, may we allow Ephesians Chapter 2 to resonate within us, reminding us that our identity in Christ encompasses and transcends every other label we may carry. In Him, we find unity amidst diversity, peace amidst strife and an unshakeable identity that the world can neither give nor take away. Stand Firm in your faith.

CHAPTER 46 MY PEOPLE ARE DESTROYED FOR LACK OF KNOWLEDGE

Okay here we go! "Ah, the story of Hosea and his wife, Comer." It's a tale of love, of faithfulness, and of an unbreakable bond between a man and his God. You see, Hosea was a man of God, a prophet who spoke the words of the Lord to the people of Israel. But little did he know, his own life would become a living testament to the power of God's love and redemption.

Gomer, his wife, was a prostitute. What? Yes, you heard that right. She was a woman who had given her body to many men, and yet, God saw fit to make her Hosea's wife. Now, you might be wondering why God would do such a thing. Why would He, the all-knowing, all-powerful God, choose a man of God to be married to a woman who had given herself to the world?

But here's the thing: God wasn't just testing Hosea's faithfulness: He was testing Corner's willingness to be redeemed. You see, Gomer was the symbol of the people of Israel, who had turned away from God and given themselves to the world. And just as Hosea loved Gomer, despite her past, God loved the people of Israel, despite their rebellion. So, Hosea took Gomer as his wife, despite her profession. And guess what? He loved her. He loved her with all his heart, just as God loved the people of Israel.

Now I know what you're thinking. This is crazy story. Why would God allow Hosea to remain married to a prostitute? Here's the thing: God wasn't just making a statement about Hosea's faithfulness; He was making a statement about His own faithfulness to Israel. You see, God is a God of second chances, of redemption and of love. So next time you feel like you've made a mistake remember Hosea and Gomer.

Wow! What an amazing story. Here is Hosea a man considered to be of high esteem. A person the people looked up to and respected. But when God wanted to highlight the children of Israel's sin to show them how ugly it looked he chose Hosea. Hosea even had to go buy his own wife back a few times. Now during these times the law was at its apex, the people had begun to question Hosea's position in God, but Hosea listened to God regardless of how the people viewed him or his wife. Hosea was determined to stick to his vows and covenant he had with god, not with the people. Hosea remained married to his cheating wife.

In Jeremiah 31:33 long before the coming of Christ, the prophet Jeremiah spoke words that would echo through the ages. "But this shall be the covenant that I will make with the house of Israel; After those days, saith the Lord, I will put my law in their inward parts, and write it in their hearts; and will be their God, and they shall be my people." This promise, serves as a corner stone of the promise of a New Covenant, one distinct from the covenant of Moses. The law would no longer exist solely on tablets of stone but would be written on the very hearts of God's people.

This scripture has been an eternal source of wisdom, guidance and prophecy for countless generations. Among the prophetic words given, those found in Jeremiah 31:33 resonate deeply with the Christian faith's foundational beliefs. This verse speaks of a profound transformation in the relationship between God and his people, a transformation heralded by the New Covenant. As we embark on an exploration of the text let's apply it the lives of the believer today. First, the essence of this prophecy hinges on a new kind of law - a law internalized and personal It is not the external adherence to commands, but the inward transformation that matters. For Christians, this means that the Holy Spirit guides them into all truth, inscribing upon their hearts a living knowledge of God's will. This resonates deeply with the Christian understanding of grace. The law is not abolished but fulfilled and made more intimate in its application.

Not every preaching, teaching or word professed in the name of religion aligns with the truth that God intends to inscribe upon our hearts. The fulfillment of Jeremiah 31:33 suggests that there is a discernment process, guided by the Holy Spirit It requires an attuned spiritual sense to distinguish which words are divinely intended for us and which are not.

Important in this discernment is that while not every message may apply directly, the principle behind it might still hold a universal truth about our relationship with God.

In the divine wisdom of God's timing, the words that resonate with our hearts are those that are most pertinent to our lived experiences and spiritual growth. As per the prophecy, the Lord writes upon our hearts in ways unique to each individuals journey. What is written may confirm, convict, guide or comfort, but it is always relevant and timely. This writing process is an ongoing one, intended to continuously draw us closer into relationship with the Creator.

Perhaps the most stunning realization about the prophecy holds true not only in our collective spiritual experience but also in our personal testimonies. For many Christians, there is a distinct moment or collection of moments when Scripture, perhaps once meaningless, becomes vibrantly alive and personally applicable. Such an understanding often comes with clarity when one is prepared to see it or in moments of profound need, affirming the truth that God's law is indeed written on our hearts.

The Word of God, understood as being Jesus Christ Himself (as depicted in John 1:1) is firmly rooted within the human heart. This joining of the Divine Word and human spirit underpin the Christian life.

The law written in our hearts is a reflection of Jesus' teachings, life and sacrifice, continuously reminding us of God's love and expectations. God's Spirit plays a crucial role in the revelation and realization of this prophecy. It is through the Spirits stirring in us that the significance of God's Word becomes apparent. The presence of the Spirit acts as both guide and interpreter, ensuring that the law written upon our hearts is understood and lived out.

Each Christian's journey in recognizing and embracing the inward law is unique. The book page serves as a testament to the promise fulfilled in the author's life - a journey that led to the writing of this book. The personal narrative is woven into the broader tapestry of Christian experience, affirming the living nature of Jeremia prophecy within believers' lives. Praise the Lord!

CHAPTER 47 THE RESURRECTION'S VERITY

In the hallowed chambers of our understanding, we find ourselves tenderly nestled within the bosom of a profound conundrum, hinged upon the veracity of the resurrection of our Savior, Jesus Christ. Could it be, as suggested by some, that Christianity, in its abiding grandeur and transformative power, is a mere tale spun by the whims of history, that Christ did not vacate that smothering tomb? For First Corinthians proclaim in the fifteenth and fourteenth verse, "And if Christ be not risen, then is our preaching vain, and our faith is also vain."

Let's delve directly knee deep, my beloved, into this theological exploration, for the resurrection of Christ is the linchpin from which our faith suspends, a pivot so crucial that without it, we are nigh unto a ship lost at sea without sail or rudder. Imagine, just for a moment, that the resurrection were but a hoax. Therewith, we remain ensnared within the coils of our iniquity, our souls bound by the transgressions. For if the resurrection is null, where then is our sacrificial lamb? For the Scripture doth declare Christ as the consummate offering, the terminus of a long lineage of temporal sacrifices-- He the Alpha and Omega of our redemption.

And ponder upon this, dear brethren: Jesus is

no creation of fable or myth. This world has crafted many a myth, but no one dare compare our Risen Lord to the fleeting fancy of a Santa Claus. A tale, when fictitious, cannot withstand the scrutinizing lens of time nor history, yet Christianity stands unwavering through ages with a vigor unmatched and untarnished. Even time itself acquiesces to His sovereignty, breaking at His birth into B.C. and A.D., history's pulse beats in rhythm with His eternal heart. A gratuitous endeavor it may seem, to follow Christ, but indeed, there is no cost in the pursuit of righteousness, and therein, a promise of everlasting life extends its hand to all who will grasp it.

Consider the valor, the sheer fortitude of the apostles, whose lives were a testament writ in the ink of sacrifice and bloodshed. These men traversed the landscape of human degeneration, not for glory or gold, but compelled by a truth they had witnessed--a truth for which they willingly bore the brunt of the world's wrath. Why, apostles were hewn in twain, decapitated, flayed, martyred in manners most gruesome, only John, it is said, succumbed to the natural wane of life's candle. Yet, he too suffered in his exile where he scribed the Revelation and his Gospel. Recall James, brother of the beloved John, seized and slain by the sword, all because he fished for men's souls, having been beckoned by the Galilean Fisherman.

My sojourners in faith, would these men, the very pillars of the Church, have stared down death, borne the lash, the chain, the edge of the executioners blade if the tomb was but a chamber for a corpse? Would the world have been set afire with the Gospel's flame if the One who claimed to be its Author remained silenced in a borrowed grave?

Nay, I say unto you, the resurrection of Jesus of Nazareth is no mere credence of a far-off hope; it is the foundation upon which stands the edifice of our salvific creed, the assured promise handed down to us from that empty sepulcher--that death has lost its sting, and life eternal reigns victorious in Christ our Lord.

In these words of faith, reflection and profound conviction, let us find courage and steadfastness in the promise of resurrection, for the Gospel is not simply a generational heirloom but a treasure of inestimable value that turns the heart from generational curses to the wealth of God's unending mercy and grace.

IN CONCLUSION

Surrender, in the conventional sense, can evoke images of defeat, of giving up control to an opposing force when all resources and power to resist are depleted. One may imagine a scenario with the police, a suspect standing cornered, hand raised in reluctant acquiescence to a power that dictates terms non-negotiable. Yet, in the Kingdom of God, surrender takes on a new dimension, a paradoxical strength found in willful vulnerability where we willingly freeze in God's presence, inviting divine scrutiny and transformation.

As we stand at the precipice of our faith, at the junction where our fear intersects with our belief, there is a gesture so profound, so ancient, and so pure that it transcends the spoken word, soaring into the realm of the spiritual. It is the act of raising our hands: a universal sign of surrender--an outward expression of an inward decision to lay down one's own striving and to submit to a will greater than ones own. When we lift our hands in the service and worship the Lord, we are signaling a surrender, an offering of ourselves to the Almighty. This act deeply woven into the fabric of our spirituality, echoes in the hallowed halls of a journey with Christ.

For our sick and suffering, the sacred act of surrender can be particularly significant. To stan before God with arms lifted is to recognize the

journey traveled, the courage mustered, and the intersectional battles fought. It is an acknowledgement
that their true allegiance lies not with the policing norms of society that might seek to constrain and define, but rather with the Creator who fearfully and wonderfully fashioned them in their mother's womb. Psalms 139:14

This surrender, lifting of hands, is an ownership of one's identity and a simultaneous acknowledgment of God's dominion over that identity. It communicates to the heavens--and to ourselves--that we are not our own, that we have been bought with a price. First Corinthians 6:19-20 and that our ultimate identity is firmly rooted in Christ. For the Christian, to lift up one's hands in worship is a deeply personal and powerful declaration that says, "Here I am, God, fully me, just as You created me. I yield not only my spirit and my heart but also my experiences, the essence of who I am-- I lay it all before You."

In the sacred act of surrender, we invite the Lord to guide our paths, to smooth the often rocky road of personal expression. It is a conscious choice to allow God's affirming voice to be louder than the whisperings of doubt or the shouts of condemnation often heard from society. It is to embrace the fullness of oneself in Christ, understanding that when we are weak in ourselves, then we are strong in the Lord. 2 Corinthians 12:10

To raise one's hands in surrender to God is simultaneously a defiance of the world's labels and limitations. It is to embody the gospel, which promises that in Christ, there is neither Jew nor Gentile, neither slave nor free, nor is there male and female, for you are all one in Christ Jesus (Galatians 3:28). In such surrender, there is a fusion of one's faith with one's lived experience., an embracing of uniqueness, and honoring the masterpiece of God's creation, which refuses to be categorized by human standards.

Indeed, to surrender is not to capitulate to an enemy, but is to join forces with the ultimate source of love, acceptance and power. It is to stand with open arms ready to receive God's boundless grace knowing that the arms that hold the universe are beckoning us into a deeper, more authentic, relationship with Him. In this act, we find that the Divine encompasses both our joys and our struggles, holding us close in an eternal embrace that seeks not to confine, but to liberate. Well family this concludes a masterpiece. If you haven't surrendered your life to Christ please do so today. May God Bless You in the Mighty Name of Jesus Amen!

ABOUT YHE AUTHOR

Gerald Bass, equipped with revelational knowledge at an early age navigated his way through the urban section of Detroit Michigan. All throughout his adult life the feds remained on his heels. His last prison stint earned him the label of "the godfather of credit card fraud" since 1986. Nevertheless, Bass persevered through this trial and tribulation and was born again in 2014. Since then he has faithfully committed himself to allowing God to use him as a living vessel to display the miraculous power of Christ. This book is of no coincidence its straight gospel from our Lord and
Savior Jesus Christ. Enjoy your reading and STAND FIRM! AMEN!

BOOK REVIEWS

WOW! WOW! WOW!
Is all I can say! But it is a lot to say about this
book. Man "G" you did this one. I joke with my brother
about how he walk and look like T.D. Jakes. Now he's
writing books just like him and no disrespect to T.D.
But this book not only felt like a letter but I was
able to read it just like that. It answered a lot of
questions and is actually an awesome read. I had to
stop myself at times so I could have more to read
tomorrow and the next and the next just couldn't put
the book down. It's one of those you wish it don't end
but like all great things it's got to come to an end.
So if you looking for a book to get you through tough
times pick up the Bible But if you looking for a good
book read this is it! Great Job Brother Gerald! People
please go grab this book!

ROBERT HENDRIX

Don't be fooled or misled by the title of this book it
is "pure gospel". It's the hottest book on the planet.
If you pass up on the opportunity to digest these
jewels that the brother continuously drop throughout
each chapter then you will miss out on the chance of a
lifetime to witness the best selling book of all times
especially for this generation. Please purchase this
book today you will not be disappointed
but properly fed and well satisfied.

CALEB NADOLSKI

I have read many books with a spiritual theme at the age of 70. However, reading this book was exceptional in its delivery G. Bass as a first time author did an excellent job, the flow of the message speak to the reader and keep them engaged, without coming off so preachy and it proselytizing. Thank You for the excellent book, I look forward to your next project. God Bless, Keep up the good work.

                              MR. CURTIS RUSSELL

www.ingramcontent.com/pod-product-compliance
Lightning Source LLC
Chambersburg PA
CBHW050649270326
41927CB00012B/2944